FIRE IN THE BELLY

An exploration of the entrepreneurial mindset

10th

Anniversary
Edition
2001-2011

Yanky Fachler

"In the end, everything depends on one's self, on a fire in the belly."
Pablo Picasso

FIRE IN THE BELLY

© 2001, 2010 Yanky Fachler

A catalogue record of this book is
available from the British Library.

ISBN 978-1-907522-21-5

Published by TAF
Printed in Ireland by Gemini International

ACKNOWLEDGEMENTS

In the Acknowledgements to the original edition of *Fire in the Belly*, I thanked Alan Clark for pushing me into the Business Start-Up field; Grainne Harte for pushing me to write the book; my wife Mona for her endless supply of support and love; my father Eli in Jerusalem and my son Ashi in California for their feedback on the manuscript; and John Teeling of Cooley Distillery for writing the foreword.

For this 10th anniversary edition of the book, I would like to add my thanks to the late Daniel R. Miller, my social psychology professor at Brunel University, who first alerted me to the distinction between the employee and entrepreneurial mindsets; Brian O'Kane of Oak Tree Press for publishing the original edition of *Fire in the Belly* and several of my other books; my son Ashi again, this time for organising the photoshoot and designing the cover; my friend and business partner in Bookbuzz, Ron Immink, for his support, honest feedback, and consistent championing of *Fire in the Belly* over the past 10 years; my sister Sue in California for providing me with the mental and physical space to do the bulk of the editing of the new edition; Dave Jones of Gemini International for helping get this edition printed and published; and Jude Torley for his wisdom and support.

I dedicate this 10th Anniversary Edition to my brother Mordechai.

Other books by Yanky Fachler

Should I, Shouldn't I (start my own business?)

My Family Doesn't Understand Me: coping strategies for entrepreneurs

Chutzpah: unlocking the maverick mindset for success

The Bookbuzz Book of Biz Book Insights 2009

The Selling Conversation, co-authored with Dermot McConkey

The Vow: rebuilding the Fachler tribe after the Holocaust

6 Officers, 2 Lions and 750 Mules

What did we do right? Global perspectives on Ireland's 'miracle'

   (chapter on enterprise and innovation)

CONTENTS

Preface to the 10th Anniversary Edition

In the autumn of 2000, shortly after I arrived in Ireland as a wordsmith for hire, I got a call from my good friend Alan Clark, Scotland's finest PR guru. He reeled off a list of my qualifications:

"You've been your own boss for over 20 years, you've spent several years strutting the amateur stage, you are instinctively enthusiastic, you're happy addressing an audience, you are critical of boring presentations, you've worked with thousands of small and medium business owner managers, and your work demands a steady stream of original and creative ideas."

"OK, I give in," I said. "What's your point?"

"It's obvious", Alan replied. "You should be motivating people who want to start their own business. Goodbye." And with that, our 90-second phone conversation was over.

Instead of calling Alan back and telling him what he could do with his ideas, I let his suggestion percolate. I then reached for the proverbial back of an envelope, and sketched out an outline for an entrepreneurial training module. The main theme of my proposal: the emotional transition that any budding entrepreneur has to make from employee status to self-employed status.

The next day, I contacted an enterprise support agency. I introduced myself as an expert in Business Start-Up, and offered my proposed "Do I Have What It Takes?" module. Serendipity smiled at me, as the agency was about to launch a Business Start-Up programme. They absorbed my module into their programme, and within days of Alan's madcap suggestion, I started delivering my training module.

Before long, I was delivering Business Start-Up workshops and seminars around Ireland, North and South, and I began receiving invitations to address national and international conferences.

A couple of months into my new career, my marketing colleague Grainne Harte said to me: "There's a book in your material." "You think so?" I asked. "Definitely," she replied.

Since it was the Christmas vacation, I sat down and wrote the manuscript for *Fire in the Belly*. Although I had written millions of words as an advertising copywriter, I had never before written a book. That's why, as a novice author, I was ignorant of the unwritten rule that you're meant to agonise and struggle over the manuscript - so I finished it within a few weeks.

My 80-year-old dad scoffed at my plan to self-publish, insisting that I contact a bona fide publisher. So I duly sent an unsolicited email to Oak Tree Press, Ireland's leading business publisher. My email read: "I've written a book that tackles a neglected aspect of the entrepreneurial equation. Are you interested?"

Brian O'Kane, the owner of Oak Tree Press, had the courtesy to email back immediately. "I have just written and published a comprehensive and definitive book about starting your own business in Ireland, and I don't think I've neglected anything." He was referring to his best-selling *Starting a New Business in Ireland*.

So I sent Brian a synopsis of my manuscript, together with a couple of sample chapters outlining my contention that too little attention is paid to the transition from employee to self-employed. Within minutes, I received an answer in my email inbox.

"Whoops, missed that!" Brian made no changes to the manuscript, and within 3 months, Oak Tree Press had published *Fire in the Belly, an exploration of the entrepreneurial spirit*. Happily, the book was very well received, and went into several printings.

The feedback I have received over the years suggests that people who are thinking about starting their own business – or thinking about thinking about starting their own business – find the book timely and useful. Since the book was first published, my views have remained as strong as ever. The book has sold consistently well since 2001, and there was a resurgence of interest in 2010, probably as a result of the recession.

Nine years after *Fire in the Belly* first appeared, Feargal Byrne warmly endorsed the book on lostjobstartbusiness.com, the website he set up to help people recently made redundant. When I eventually met Feargal, he told me that his degree in Marketing and Entrepreneurship had left him totally unprepared for the actual experience of becoming an entrepreneur. Feargal claimed he read things in *Fire in the Belly* that no one had ever mentioned in all the years he studied entrepreneurship.

A similar sentiment was expressed in an email I received from another entrepreneurship graduate:

"Here's food for thought. Last year, I completed my MBA at a prestigious university. I find it both ironic and absurd that the issues that you tackle, about what it takes or what it means to be an entrepreneur, were never even touched upon during my studies. When you think about it, this kind of discussion should be a basic part of any MBA. After all, you're dealing with people some of whom – me included - see themselves as future entrepreneurs. What planet are these business schools on?"

Encouraged by the fact that the message of *Fire in the Belly* remains as relevant as ever, I decided to produce this 10th anniversary edition, published by TAF. I have updated some of the case studies, and I have ironed out some of the typos in the original (and doubtlessly introduced a few new ones!)

I have also expanded on two themes that later became books in their own right: the myth of family support (*My Family Doesn't*

Understand Me); and the need for a ballsy attitude (*Chutzpah: Unlocking the maverick mindset for Success.*)

This new edition of *Fire in the Belly,* like the original, seeks to supplement, not replace, conventional Business Start-Up training. I leave others more qualified, like Brian O'Kane and Ron Immink, to write about the nuts and bolts of entrepreneurship - the practical steps needed to start and grow a new business.

I see my contribution as directing the spotlight squarely on the entrepreneurial mindset. I want to reach the parts of the entrepreneur's soul that other books forget.

I want to see what it takes emotionally to start your own business.

I want to see who should, and who shouldn't, start their own business.

CHAPTER 1
Off the Ladder
and Up the Wall

Leaving your salaried job to start your own business is in vogue. More people than ever are actively considering the entrepreneurial route.

George W. Bush may not have known that entrepreneur was a French word, but he knew that entrepreneurs play a vital role as an engine for job creation and driving economic growth. "Without entrepreneurs," he told the Small Business Association, "the American dream would go unrealised."

The ladder in the title of this chapter refers to the career ladder, the world of salaried employment. The people who inhabit this world are ladder people. After I started adopting the ladder metaphor in my Business Start-Up workshops, I found that participants really warmed to ladder terminology. Ever since, I have brought a real ladder along to all my talks. (This has caused confusion among over-zealous maintenance staff. They see a step ladder standing in the middle of the room before I start, assume it was left there by mistake, and try to remove it.)

To become an entrepreneur, you must by definition get off the ladder.

The wall in the chapter title refer to the fact that people all around you will tell you that you must be up the wall to consider starting your own business. You must be crazy.

Did you know that at some stage of their career, 80%-90% of all salaried employees fantasise about starting their own business? Apparently, a lot more people than we realise are considering making the jump.

However, only a relatively small minority of the fantasists actually give up their employee status to start their own business.

> *"Do or do not. There is no try."*
> Yoda in Star Wars

For this minority, there is no shortage of helpful resources to choose from. There are thousands of entrepreneurship websites; hundreds of "How to start your own business" books; national and local enterprise support agencies; training organizations offering SYOB programmes; and entrepreneurial consultants.

Do I have any argument with the need to impart entrepreneurial advice?

Of course not.

But......

As you will discover, when it comes to the actual decision to start your own business, nearly all of these entrepreneurial resources only pay lip service to the entrepreneurial mindset. What they really want to do is get down to the business of helping you master the required entrepreneurial skills.

Some SYOB books totally ignore the decision to become an entrepreneur. Others devote a few sentences, a few paragraphs, or even a whole chapter to the subject.

But the dominant theme running through most books, websites and training programmes is:

"You want to be your own boss? Great, we can teach you the critical skills you need to start your own business."

By skills, they mean entrepreneurial skills, business skills, time management skills, people skills, marketing skills, funding skills, tax-related skills, and the skills required to profitably develop, market and deliver a new product or service.

In other words, there is an underlying assumption that the decision to be your own boss is pretty straightforward. The more difficult stage is to successfully master the skills for running your own business.

Wrong!

It's the other way round.

Addressing what you have to **do** to start your own business, before looking at what you have to **be**, is putting the cart before the horse.

Before you address the **what** and the **how** of entrepreneurship, you should address something more fundamental – the **why**.

- **Why** do you want to jump off the ladder in the first place?
- **Why**, if you're not happy at your place of work, don't you look for another position somewhere else?
- **Why** do you want to start your own business?

The critical – and difficult - part is deciding whether you have what it takes to become an entrepreneur. Once you make that decision, I believe that anyone of average intelligence can master the required skills.

Can you successfully make the emotional transition – as opposed to the physical or logical transition - from the ladder world to the non-ladder world? That's the real question.

Pumping people full of entrepreneurial skills, knowledge, facts and tips serves little purpose unless we first conduct an audit on their suitability to be entrepreneurs.

This book is dedicated to this neglected part of the entrepreneurial equation.

There are some who question whether it is possible to teach entrepreneurship in the first place. I got into hot water after I wrote an article in the Journal of the Institute of Business Advisors: "Entrepreneurial training – red herring?" I was accused of undermining the very basis of entrepreneurial education.

The point I was making is that entrepreneurial skills are only part of the story. If the entrepreneurial mindset is right, I believe it is possible to learn entrepreneurial skills. If the mindset isn't right, then entrepreneurial skills won't help anyway.

Have you noticed that everything we have said so far in this chapter assumes that we all start out as employees?

Is this a safe assumption? Absolutely.

To prove it, think about how many people you know who skipped the employee stage, and went straight from the educational system to self-employment.

Very few, if any. Why? Because 99.99% of us start our working career working for someone else. It's what the educational system requires of us.

There are all sorts of reasons why we attend school: To learn. To gain knowledge. To get an education. To learn social skills, communication skills and sports skills. To learn values. To expand our minds. To get qualifications. Because the law forces us to go to school, and because our parents want us to go to school.

But the main reason we go to school has precious little to do with expanding our minds or learning values.

We go to school because society needs a steady supply of employable citizens.

We go to school as part of society's policy of urging us, training us, cajoling us, pushing us and expecting us to become employees.

The result of this mass brainwashing exercise is that the vast majority of kids that go through the education system do indeed emerge as employable citizens.

And when we say employable, we always mean employees, not self-employed!

A well-orchestrated chorus of parents, teachers, faith leaders, the media, business leaders and the government bangs home the same message that school is our passport to a career as loyal employees. We go to school in order to get a job.

And getting a job means security, stability, regular salary, career prospects, pension, and other social benefits.

In other words, getting a job means getting a ladder job.

Almost to a person, we buy into this 'go to work for someone else' model. We work hard to get the qualifications – school leaving certificate, university degree, diploma and the like – that allow us to apply for a job.

The magic letter or email of acceptance arrives, and we proudly turn up at an office, shop, plant or other place of employment on our first day at work.

As we do so, we are taking our first step on the first rung of the career ladder.

We join the ladder world.

We become ladder people.

A stark illustration of this programming was provided by Jenifer, a participant in one of my workshops. Here is her description of her young son's first day at school.

When Pete came home from school, I asked him how his day had been. "Fine, mum," he replied. His father entered the room. Pulling himself to his full height, he towered over Pete. "Son," he said, "Do you realise that today you began a life sentence of hard labour? From today and for the next 10 years, you're going to be doing hard labour at school. For the following 45 years you're going to be doing hard labour at work. Not much of a life to look forward to, is it son?"

All educational systems train, condition and brainwash us to become employees. According to Sir Ken Robinson, author of *The Element*, and the star of a much-downloaded 18-minute presentation to the TED conference in 2006, all public education systems were designed to fit the world of the Industrial Revolution – 200 years ago!

The educational system is no longer fit for purpose, says Robinson.

My view on all this is clear and unambiguous: Society brainwashes us to become employees.

So anyone wishing to jump off the ladder must undergo debriefing, debugging and deprogramming.

Anyone who wants to jump off the ladder has to ditch the employee mindset.

Case Study

John Taylor Gatto won the 1991 New York City Teacher of the Year award. But he was a frustrated man. He believed that the school curriculum was stifling kids' imagination and their natural development. He decided to use the awards ceremony to make his point. This is what he told the audience of educators:

"The only reason I've been a great teacher for my students is because I didn't do a single thing you told me to. I ignored your 'standards,' I thwarted your bureaucracy and I taught unauthorized material. I filled out those forms that said the students were in their desks, when they were really taking horizon-expanding study trips. I had them read real books instead of those inane, dumbed-down textbooks of yours, I taught them real history instead of the porridge of revisionist pabulum you call 'social studies'. Your bureaucracy is a mill that grinds up human beings and turns them into consumer fertilizer for a planned economy. Human potential erodes as hungry minds sit in listless boredom, and teachers operate without the tools they need. Most of your students can't read after 12 years of education - even though it only takes 3 months to learn how to read. That's why most kids follow the herd into a bleak future instead of thinking for themselves."

After delivering this slashing attack, Gatto officially announced his resignation, and wrote an op ed page in the Wall Street Journal in which he claimed that he was no longer willing to hurt children.

Unless people first understand at a personal level, at a feelings level and at an emotional level what starting a business involves, I see little point in exposing them to a battery of entrepreneurial skills.

We are designed, weaned, trained from Day One to be productive members of society. And we are heavily guilted into believing that this must involve some sort of droning repetitive pod-like dress-coded work for a larger corporate cause."
Mark Morford

I always think of jumping off the ladder as being like Alcoholics Anonymous, the famous organisation that helps wean recovering alcoholics off the drinking mindset. Maybe we need an Employees Anonymous organisation to help wean recovering employees off the employee mindset.

I got into a blazing argument when I used the term "recovering employees" during a discussion of *Fire in the Belly* with a group of bankers. I was trying to get them to understand the mindset of the entrepreneurs who come knocking on their doors looking for loans.

"Do you mean to say," thundered one irate banker, "that being an employee is a sickness that the self-employed need to be cured of?" "I couldn't have put it better myself," I replied.

Does my emphasis on the emotional transition from the ladder to the non-ladder world guarantee your business will prosper?

No!

Anyone who makes such a claim is hoodwinking you. There is no guarantee. However strong your desire to be your own boss, no one can guarantee you success. However many books you read, and however many training programmes you attend, an entrepreneurial mindset alone may not be enough. In the real world, many different factors can conspire to bring even the most viable business venture to its knees.

But focussing exclusively on the risks of starting a business is to miss the very essence of the entrepreneurial experience.

In this book, we will explore why people swap the so-called "security" of the employment world for the so-called "insecurity" of being your own boss. We will explore the differences between a world where someone else decides how you spend your working hours, and a world where you decide your own priorities.

Some employees should never be tempted to get off the ladder. Others should never have been on the ladder in the first place. Some self-employed people should never have left employment, while others discover a fulfilment in entrepreneurship that they never felt when they were on the ladder.

And many people on or off the ladder will spend a lifetime wondering if they are in the right place. Or wondering if they have leaned their ladder against the right wall.

Case Study

Paul gave up his job as a manager in an electronics company, and used his woodworking talents to build and sell high quality dog kennels. He had done his market research and attended a Business Start-Up course, and was about to launch his business when he received a fabulous offer from another electronics plant. They offered him a huge salary increase, almost total autonomy, his own team, a great pension, everything. He was very tempted. It was in this confused state that Paul attended my workshop. At the end of the evening, he shared with us his dilemma: "It was only when I watched you climbing up and down that ladder, and heard you describe how people feel when they are on and when they are off, that I realised that I am more scared of getting back on a ladder again than I am of starting my own business." Paul resisted the temptation to take the ladder job. His kennel business is now thriving, and he has branched out into garden sheds and - would you believe it - ladders.

I use the word explore deliberately. Explore, not judge. I do not divide the world into goodies (non-ladder people) and baddies (ladder people). I make no claim that the ladder world is all bad, or that the non-ladder world is all good. And while I try to openly encourage anyone who wants to take the entrepreneurial route, I acknowledge that this route is not for everyone.

A young man told me after a workshop: "You have convinced me never to start my own business." "Then I've done you a favour," I replied. "I've probably saved you a heap of money that would have been swallowed up by a venture you should never have started."

Becoming your own boss is never a straightforward rational decision.

It's a leap of faith.

It's as much about emotional as financial independence.

It's about embarking on an adventure.

Ultimately, asking whether entrepreneurship is for you is the wrong question.

The real question is whether you are right for entrepreneurship.

Join me as we try and see what makes entrepreneurs tick.

CHAPTER 2

Entrepreneurship – A Question of Definition

"Going into business for yourself, becoming an entrepreneur, is the modern-day equivalent of pioneering on the old frontier."
Paula Nelson

Everyone admires the entrepreneur. But what exactly is an entrepreneur?

There is surprisingly little consensus. Every entrepreneurial expert seems to offer a different definition.

The Merriam-Webster dictionary tells us that an entrepreneur is "someone who organizes, manages, and assumes the risks of a business or enterprise."

The University of Rochester defines entrepreneurship as "transforming an idea into an enterprise that generates value."

The Kauffman Center for Entrepreneurial Leadership defines an entrepreneur as "someone who is willing and eager to create a new venture in order to present a concept to the marketplace, someone who creates and manages change by pursuing opportunity, acting with passion for a purpose, living proactively, and leveraging resources to create value."

Some entrepreneurship experts distinguish between the old definition of entrepreneurship: "The process for starting a new business"; and the new definition: "An opportunistic mindset and spirit."

Others distinguish between "true entrepreneurs" who are driven by opportunity, focus on innovation, are determined to create new value by shaking up the marketplace, and are determined to grow; and "lifestyle businesses" that "simply" want to provide a job for themselves and to provide income for their family.

I don't think that this petty approach does justice to people who want to start their own business, but who don't necessarily want to build an empire.

Maybe we're talking about the different ways in which Americans and Europeans define an entrepreneur. Americans tend to assume that success alone determines whether or not a person is an entrepreneur. If you are not a fantastic success story, you don't have the right to call yourself an entrepreneur.

To confuse the issue further, entrepreneurship is often used to describe other areas of life, including intrapreneurship see p.   )

Personally, I like the following definitions:

"A corporate mutineer."

"The skydivers of the business world. The thrill of the jump is almost as important as the safe landing."

But for the purposes of this book, we will use a simple working definition:

> **"An entrepreneur is anyone driven by an urge to get off the ladder in order to create a viable business."**

Hopefully, this definition will fit most people who want to start their own business. This definition includes high tech, low tech and no tech. It includes people who want to work in services or in manufacturing. It includes people who want to work on their own (soloists) and those who intend to build major undertakings involving huge investments and the creation of many jobs. It includes bricks 'n mortar operations, click 'n order operations, and bricks 'n clicks operations.

So far, we have posed two contrasting worlds: the employment world (the ladder world) and the world of self-employment (the non-ladder world.)

This assumes a clear and self-evident distinction between employee and self-employed. If you work under the same roof as your employer, you're an employee. If you work under your own roof, you are self-employed.

However, the shifting sands of the employment world are blurring these traditional distinctions. There is not even a universal statutory definition of employee/self-employed. Income tax authorities around the world have different definitions of employment status.

Obvious tell-tale signs such as being registered for VAT, paying contributions to social insurance or being registered as a business name, are no longer sufficient to determine whether someone is employed or self-employed.

The distinction is also complicated by the fact that you can be an employee of one employer, but a self-employed contractor for another employer.

You can be employed part-time by an employer, while at the same time you are a part-time self-employed consultant with your own business.

You can work under the same roof as an employer but be self-employed, and you can work from home but still be an employee.

Nevertheless, there's a fundamental distinction between the ladder and non-ladder worlds. This table offers some rule-of-thumb distinguishing principles.

You are probably **ON THE LADDER** if you can answer 'YES' to all of the following questions:	You are probably **OFF THE LADDER** if you can answer 'YES' to all of the following questions:
• Can someone tell you at any time what to do? • Can someone tell you at any time where, when and how to carry out the work? • Do you work a set amount of hours? • Can someone move you from task to task? • Are you paid by the hour, week, or month? • Can you get overtime pay or bonus payment? • Are you managed within a logical corporate hierarchy? • Can you look forward to the prospect of steady promotion if you perform adequately? • Is your job at the mercy of others?	• Can you hire someone to do the work at your own expense? • Are you risking your own money, and do you alone control the opportunity for profit or loss from your work? • Do you agree on a fixed price regardless of how long the job may take? • Can you determine what work to do, how and when to do the work and where to provide the services? • Do you regularly accept work from more than one client? • Do you have to correct unsatisfactory work in your own time and at your own expense? • Are you responsible for paying your own income taxes? • Do you invoice your clients for work completed?

CHAPTER 3
The Ladder World

The ladder world as we know it only emerged about 200 years ago with the industrial revolution, and reached its peak in the 1950s and 1960s, when corporate culture dominated western capitalist thinking.

In ancient times, there were very few ladders. We were farmers, merchants, fishermen, carpenters, stone-masons, healers, boat builders, weavers, innkeepers, scribes, potters, bakers, spinners, tanners, perfumers and goldsmiths. We learned a trade and sold our expertise or our goods. We were entrepreneurs.

The corporate culture that has dominated western capitalist thinking for two centuries, considers working on a ladder as the norm. In the USA and eventually in most other modern societies, the culture of corporate conformity defined the way you dressed, the people you mingled with, and where you took your vacations.

(Brian): "You are all individuals"
(Crowd): "We are all individuals".
(Lone voice from the back): "I'm not!"
Life of Brian

There was a clear and powerful message: Don't mess with the ladder world. According to this mentality, the only serious business is big business. The only real players in the business world are the major corporations.

The logical accompaniment of this was an assumption in the business world that as corporations got bigger, the justification for small businesses would disappear.

Some mega-organisations still regard even the smallest entrepreneur as a threat. Major corporations flex their muscles against much smaller businesses, as this story shows.

Case Study

Entrepreneur Media is the publisher of Entrepreneur Magazine, a highly successful publication in the USA that has been a great source of inspiration to many entrepreneurs. Astonishingly, Entrepreneur Media has sued dozens of companies and websites that had the temerity to use the word "entrepreneur." A court awarded Entrepreneur Media over £250,000 damages against a PR company that called itself EntrepreneurPR. Ironically, Entrepreneur Media even sues successful small businesses featured in Entrepreneur Magazine. They sued Stardock for selling a computer game called Entrepreneur. Stardock's CEO said that the whole thing reminded him of a scene in the movie Independence Day. The President asks the alien: "What do you want us to do?" The alien replies: "Die." If Entrepreneur Media succeeds in its campaign to stamp out all smaller competitors who use the word entrepreneur, I wonder whether they will demand that I pulp all copies of Fire in the belly.

Predictions that only big business would survive have proved wrong. The ladder world now recognises that a healthy economy is one where more and more entrepreneurs are setting up their own business.

We all start our working career on the ladder. As soon as we acclimatise to our surroundings, we set about building our career, our sights firmly set on moving up to the next rung of the ladder. And the next rung. And the next. Very few people have zero ambition. Very few people want to remain on the bottom rung for the rest of their employment career.

Many people feel good about joining the ladder world. They enjoy their work, they enjoy their work environment.

Some people go to extraordinary lengths to land a particular job.

After studying in drama school, Clare Booth Luce became a homemaker until her marriage ended. She set her heart on working for fashion magazine Vogue, and successfully secured a job interview with Vogue publisher Conde Nast. But he did not offer her a job.

Clare refused to accept that this meant that she wasn't going to work at Vogue. So she turned up at the Vogue office, and informed an assistant that she had been hired. She found a vacant desk, and sat at it. By the time Nast realised what had happened, Clare had made herself invaluable. She was quickly promoted to editorial assistant, and within four years she had gone from uninvited walk-in to editor.

Tony Stevens was a 13-year-old orphan who left school to join the Merchant Navy in 1939. At the end of WW2, he looked for a job on dry land at a time when the employment market was suffering from a glut of demobilised servicemen. He walked into a small engineering firm in London, and literally begged the boss to give him a job. The boss turned Tony down on the grounds that he was not qualified. Tony burst into copious tears, and sobbingly pleaded to be given an opportunity to prove himself. The boss relented, Tony was taken on, and later became a captain of industry.

These tactics might not work in today's work environment, but they show what determination can achieve.

What happens if you don't like your ladder job? No worries. You simply hop off one ladder and hop on to another one. Being wedded to the ladder world does not mean that you always like your particular ladder. In normal economic times, you can always look for another ladder that offers you a job more to your liking.

There are all sorts of reasons why people change ladders. Not getting on with a boss or with colleagues. Finding the work boring.

Lack of career advancement. A belief that another ladder will pay more. Seeking greater responsibility. Hoping to make better use of your skills and talents.

Ladder hopping is perfectly legitimate - and perfectly normal. Everyone does it. How many people have you ever met who only ever worked for one employer? Globally, employee churn is rising. People are staying a shorter time in their jobs. Ladder hopping is merely a form of corrective action. Eventually, most employees find their equilibrium, and settle on a ladder than suits them.

If you're happy to be a ladder person, good luck to you. Don't think about changing who you are and what you do. It can be very motivating to move up the career ladder. And don't let me or any other entrepreneurship expert deter you from continuing along the path you have chosen.

Ladder people don't need to apologise. To quote my California-based son Ashi (who describes himself as a fourth entrepreneur), "Some of my best friends are ladder people." I would never urge anyone to jump off the ladder just because others are doing it. Don't leave the ladder world unless and until you are sure that this is what you want to do.

Not that everyone on the ladder necessarily sees the ladder world through rose-tinted glasses.

Psychoanalyst Corinne Maier, a French civil servant, wrote a best-seller called *Bonjour Paresse* (Hello Laziness). This part satire, part manifesto for bored and disgruntled workers ("a graceful attack on the corporate world" - The Village Voice) describes corporate culture as the "crystallisation of the stupidity of a group of people at a given moment."

The book offers tongue-in-cheek subversive tips for looking productive without actually doing anything. Keep a low profile. Don't stand out from the crowd. Don't volunteer. Don't make waves. Don't over-perform. Don't complain. Learn to be a cog in a bigger machine. Seek out the most useless positions.

"I'd rather be my own general than a loyal corporate foot soldier"
Michael Bloomberg

Another rant against the ladder world appears in *Why Work Sucks – and how to fix it*, by Cali Ressler and Jody Thompson, who claim that our outdated beliefs about work are based on assumptions that do not apply in today's 24/7 economy. Here are some excerpts:

- We go to work and give everything we have and are treated like we're children who, if left unattended, will steal candy.
- We go to work and watch someone who isn't very good at their job get promoted because they got in earlier and stayed later than anyone else.
- We go to work and sit through overlong, overstaffed meetings to talk about the next overlong, overstaffed meeting.
- We see talented, competent, productive people get penalised for having kids, for not being good at office politics, for being a little different.

Management guru Peter Drucker, who knew a thing or two about the ladder world, claimed that paid jobs were too risky because they destroy people's creativity with routine and limits.

Management literature in recent years talks about the growing phenomenon of presenteeism, a term used to describe people who show up to work, but do not perform to their capacity. Presenteeism is closely related to employee disengagement. Disengaged employees are not emotional committed to their work. They come to work, they do what they are asked to do and they don't do more than required. They don't make suggestions for improving processes or work methods. They don't offer up any new ideas. They are not emotionally involved.

Even the International Labour Organisation acknowledges that there is a growing feeling that the dignity of work has been devalued, that it is seen as simply a factor of production – a commodity – forgetting the individual, family, community and national significance of human work.

Bob Black, in *The Abolition of Work*, claims that people who are regimented all their lives, handed to work from school and bracketed by the family in the beginning and the nursing home at the end, are habituated to hierarchy and psychological enslavement. Their obedience training at work carries over into the families they start, thus reproducing the system.

In this chapter, we looked at the people who inhabit the ladder world – whether willingly or unwillingly.

In the next chapter, we will look at what happens when people no longer wish to inhabit the ladder world.

CHAPTER 4
When ladders become a health hazard

"I am the kind of guy who kept getting spat out of the corporate world. I just couldn't fit in anywhere."
Copywriter John Carlton

What happens when you no longer regard working for someone else as part of your life plan?

What happens when you experience entrepreneurial stirrings?

What happens when you hear an internal voice telling you that there is an alternative to the ladder world?

What happens when after years of accepting the rules and expectations of the ladder world, you reach the sad conclusion that you don't really like it there?

In short, what happens when you want to jump off the ladder?

For many people who face these questions before they are 18, the educational system can be a disaster. Schools do not encourage us to do our own thing. Entrepreneurship rarely figures in any school curriculum. Schools do not see their role as encouraging us to opt out of the workforce, to desert the ladder world of which schools themselves are such an essential part.

No surprise then that so many successful entrepreneurs dropped out of an educational system that failed to hold much interest for people who think differently.

Well-known school dropout Richard Branson describes school as "a place where grown-ups were just trying to keep us busy." Other dropouts include Soichiro Honda, Vidal Sassoon, Mark Twain, Thomas Edison, Charlie Chaplin, Freddy Laker, Albert Einstein, Agatha Christie, Cher and Milton Hershey.

The entrepreneurial urge grabs us when we discover that it's not this ladder or that ladder that we don't like.

We realise that we don't like ladders. Period.

> *"I don't think I've ever been very comfortable working within an organisation. I don't think I was cut out to bide my time and work my way up the ladder, so I looked for an opportunity to be my own boss."*
> Kate Beasedale, head of Sinclair Montrose Healthcare

Some lucky people have always known that they were entrepreneurs. They have always known that unless they work for themselves, they will always be miserable. They have always been obsessed with the idea of being their own boss.

I say lucky, because at least they know that their sojourn in the ladder world is a temporary one.

For others, it may take longer to reach this conclusion. That's what happened with me. I never thought I had entrepreneurial potential.

I remember listening to Professor Dan Miller in Brunel University as he discussed the differences between children raised in a home where one or both parents were self-employed (non-ladder children), and children whose parents worked for someone else (ladder children). Miller divided the world into Entrepreneurs and Bureaucrats. Entrepreneurial parents tend to have entrepreneurial children, because these children absorb the cultural norms of their independent, entrepreneurial parents. Homes where "business" and "being your own boss" have positive connotations, can encourage children to go it alone.

The home environment of Bureaucratic (ladder) families, says Miller, does not encourage children to seek independent non-ladder jobs. Children in ladder families are more likely to follow the example of their employee parents. Ladder children can learn to look down on entrepreneurs, profit, success and excess industriousness.

Miller's Bureaucrat/Entrepreneur theory obviously made a lasting impression on me, and is the root of my ladder/non-ladder views. But at the time, I remember thinking: I like the theory, but it does not fit my personal experience.

My dad hated every minute of his early years as an employee. He fled from the ladder world at the first opportunity, and had been his own boss since I was 6 years old. The whole household revolved around his retail food service business. He was a typical owner manager of a small enterprise. He always brought work home, he worked long hours, he quietly worried 24/7 about his business.

According to Miller, I should have absorbed entrepreneurial stimuli and entrepreneurial values at home. I should have developed an entrepreneurial mindset.

But I didn't.

The thought never crossed my mind. I was 20, studying for my first degree, and looking forward to graduating and getting a ladder job. I was sure that I shared none of my father's entrepreneurial spirit.

After completing my first and second degrees (everyone told me that I would go further in the ladder world with an MA), I joined the ladder world with gusto. My first job was on the lowest rung of a ladder - a university researcher.

On my next ladder, I had a more prestigious title: management consultant.

On another ladder I was near the top, as Deputy Managing Director of a small electronics company.

On every ladder, I performed well. I did what I was paid to do. But something wasn't right. I realised that I wasn't happy in any ladder job.

It took me a while – several years, in fact - to acknowledge this. In the pit of my stomach, I started getting a nagging feeling that working for someone else was not what I wanted. I felt a growing mismatch between my performance and my soul.

Eventually, after I had worked my way through several ladder jobs, I concluded that ladder life was not for me.

I realised that I had inherited my dad's entrepreneurial virus after all.

And just like a computer virus, once an entrepreneurial virus attacks the system, it can cause havoc. It gets into the brain, into the heart, into the soul – and into the belly. And once that happens, you have to do something, unless you want to spend the rest of your life asking "What if...?"

> *"The saddest summary of a life contains three descriptions: could have, might have, and should have."*
> Louis E. Boone

Once you are attacked by this virus, you become a liability to the ladder world. You become unfit to work under any boss.

That was my story. I came to believe that in every employment situation, my boss would turn out to be a jerk. By definition, no boss would ever appreciate my talents.

I reached the conclusion that ladders were bad for my health. In practice, I became unemployable. And when you are unemployable, you are already halfway off the ladder.

"I'm a bad employee and need to build my own castles in the air."
Richard Koch

When the Roman senate ordered Julius Caesar to relinquish control of the armies he had commanded as governor in Gaul in 49 BCE, Caesar retaliated by invading Italy. But when he reached the Rubicon River on the border between Gaul and Italy, he paused.

Do I cross into Roman territory or not?

Uttering the words: "Jacta alea est" (The die is cast), he eventually overcame his scruples. He crossed his Rubicon. He passed the tipping point.

Realising that ladders are bad for your health is undoubtedly your own personal Rubicon. The die is cast as you give up the four solid legs of the ladder in order to stand on your own two feet.

And it can be scary. And exciting. Both at the same time.

The next thing that has to happen is something that triggers your departure from the ladder world. The next chapter looks at some of these triggers.

"Leaving nice co-workers, a stable paycheck, and 12 years of tenure with one company was the scariest thing I'd ever done. And yet looking back, it was the defining moment of my career."
Michael J. Katz, founder, Blue Penguin Development

CHAPTER 5

What triggers can push us or pull us off the ladder?

During my work with thousands of aspiring entrepreneurs, I have found it useful to distinguish between two types of triggers: those that push us and those that pull us off the ladder.

- PUSH TRIGGERS: The stimulus comes from inside you, and pushes you to embark on the entrepreneurial path.

- PULL TRIGGERS: Something from the outside pulls you towards starting your own business.

1. FRUSTRATION

Frustration with the ladder world is one of the most frequently cited push triggers.

I divide frustration into practical, emotional/philosophical and authority-related factors.

Practical factors that can cause frustration include unhappiness with your slow progress up the promotional ladder. You may resent the long commute to work. You may object when others take credit for your ideas, you may want to work the hours that suit your individual body clock, and you may object making money for someone else.

Emotional/philosophical factors can cause this frustration. You may not feel fulfilled at work. You may feel you have no scope for personal growth. You may find your work boring and mindless. You may believe that you cannot express your creativity.

Authority-related factors can cause this frustration. You may be impatient with the rules and regulations. You may dislike being at the whim of your manager. You may not like being nagged. You may want to be master of your own schedules, agendas, time and pace.

Sometimes this frustration can be apparent very quickly, sometimes it's a slow burn:

Case Studies

- *Damon Dash, head of the Roc-A-Fella Records empire, always knew he wanted to be his own boss. Bill Gates was his role model. He got his first job in a deli when he was 14. On the first day, he was told to deliver something. His reaction was: "I'm not taking orders from anyone." After less than an hour in the ladder world, Damon had enough and walked out.*

- *Howard Pau arrived in Britain at the age of 17 from China, and by the age of 35, he had a good job as a Post Office engineer. His promotion prospects looked good. One day, his supervisor held a retirement party after 43 years of service. Management had allowed him to invite 50 colleagues, but 70 people actually turned up. The following day, when the supervisor arrived at work, he was presented with a music system as a retirement gift – and a bill for the extra 20 people who had attended the party. Howard was shocked, depressed and disillusioned. "Am I going to wait for my music centre or am I going to make my own destiny?" He realised that the ladder world no longer appealed to him. So he opened Ireland's first store specialised in supplying Asian foods to restaurants. And all because of the mean-spiritedness of the Post Office management.*

2. MONEY TO SPARE OR THE LURE OF HIGH EARNINGS

Circumstances can suddenly place a sizeable amount of money at your disposal. You win the lottery. A great-aunt you never heard of bequeaths you money in her will. You receive a substantial early-retirement pay-out. You make a killing on the stock market. Your horse comes in at 100:1.

Insufficient funding often accounts for businesses failure. So isn't starting out without having to source external financing a good thing?

Not necessarily.

Starting a new business just because you have the financial ability to do so is not a good enough reason to leave the ladder world. Entrepreneurship is not just about money. It's better to be pulled along by a dream, than to be pushed along by a money pot.

If the sudden availability of money can act as a powerful push trigger, so too can the prospect of high earnings act as a powerful pull trigger. Many employees who resent toiling away making money for someone else, start looking to self-employment as a way of redressing this.

But there is an important question you have to ask yourself: What happens if despite your best efforts, you don't end up earning more off the ladder than you earned on the ladder? Does that mean that you failed?

Looking for a fast track to a fast buck can backfire. Surveys that explore the complex motivations of people who start businesses tell us that the desire for autonomy and control consistently outranks wealth.

"I had no ambition to make a fortune. Mere money-making has never been my goal, I had an ambition to build."
John D. Rockefeller

According to the National Federation of Small Business Owners, less than 20% of the current business owners started a business for money.

Very few of the thousands of participants in my workshops claim to have been attracted by huge potential earnings.

Don't get me wrong. I would love to see every aspiring entrepreneur driving a Ferrari. I would love to see every self-employed person buy a magnificent house and live a life of luxury. But the lure of money alone is not a safe enough trigger to start your own business. High earnings should be the benefit – not the goal - of working for yourself.

Case Study

Jenny had married well. Her husband's family had a huge house, they took trips and cruises, and the children went to the best private schools. Jenny came from a less wealthy background. Her father was a civil servant, and had risen to chief clerk in the Town Hall. Jenny had a degree in marketing, and happily accepted her father-in-law's offer to work in the research department of his investment bank. Intoxicated by the vast amounts of money flowing through the bank, Jenny pestered her father-in-law to lend her $2 million in order to set up her own portfolio management company. Overjoyed with being her own boss, Jenny did what she had seen every boss do. She bought beautiful offices. She hired great-looking staff. She had a great car. She enjoyed long lunches. The one thing she didn't do was devote her efforts to her business. Unsurprisingly, her business folded within a few months. The money had enticed her, but she didn't have what it takes to start, run and grow a successful business.

3. TRAUMATIC EVENT

Sometimes, adversity and trauma that are unconnected with getting fired can provide the stimulus for an entrepreneurial career. College drop-out Vickie Stringer fell for a drug dealer who disappeared after getting her pregnant. She continued to deal drugs, and was making $30,000 a week when she sold cocaine to a police informant, and was sentenced to 5 years in a federal penitentiary.

Three months before she got out of jail, she felt a strong urge to tell her story, and within a few weeks she had completed the manuscript of a fictionalised story of her life, "Let That Be the Reason." She was a 29-year-old felon with no degree, no résumé, no money and no prospects. While trying to find a publisher, she got a job as a bartender at Columbus Airport. 26 rejection slips later, Vickie decided to self-publish, and raised enough funds from family and friends to print 2,500 copies, selling her book door-to-door.

One of her customers in the bar showed the manuscript to a publisher that offered her $50,000. The book eventually sold over 100,000 copies. Vickie started her own publishing company. In a few short years, she had gone from drug queen to owner of a $1.8 million company.

4. GETTING FIRED

Getting fired is the mother of all push triggers - because you are quite literally pushed off your ladder. There are all sorts of fancy names for getting fired: Being downsized, being made redundant, getting canned, early retirement, last in first out, being dismissed, being let go, being terminated.

But the bottom line is the same: You're toast. One day you can be happy in your safe and secure job with a blue-chip employer, and you wake up the next day to hear (often in the media) that your secure job has vanished.

In this era of increasing globalisation, thousands of jobs can be lost in an instant. All it takes is for an employer to discover an alternative, cheaper source of labour somewhere else in the world. Someone on the other side of the world pressed a button – and you're history. You're the weakest link. Goodbye. You have been pushed off the ladder, whether you like it or not.

Entrepreneurship is not an automatic solution for everyone who gets fired. If you are fired because of a personality clash with your superior or your boss, look for a better job with a better boss on a different ladder.

David Jones in *Oh No, I've lost my job*, says that losing your job is one of the most harrowing things that can happen to you. It ranks alongside bereavement and divorce as one of the major traumas that can have a negative impact on your life. And it leads to a feeling of anger, confusion, fear, embarrassment and shame. You feel sorry for yourself, you worry about keeping up your payments on the house, and there are ego issues.

If losing your job comes as a total surprise, there is a temptation to choose the entrepreneurial route as a kind of revenge. Avoid this temptation! Just as having funds is not in itself sufficient reason to jump off the ladder, so making big decisions about your future when you are vulnerable is not a great idea either.

Imagine you are the passenger in a car driven by someone suffering from Road Rage. How much to you trust the driver's reactions? It's the same with starting your own business. Doing it because you're angry may not be a trustworthy response.

So be honest with yourself. If your first instinct after being fired is to start out on your own, ask yourself whether you are acting on the rebound. Can you trust your reactions? Did you get fired because you wanted to be fired? Are you tempted to start your own business out of desperation or out of excitement?

Which is not to say that you should never start a new business after being fired. If you have long dreamed, schemed and planned for this moment, being told that you no longer have a job could be a blessing in disguise.

Some "necessity entrepreneurs" do successfully convert a high-octane cocktail of raw emotions into a powerful entrepreneurial pursuit.

Case Study

Australian-born Wendy Pye was a go-getting divisional manager for the NZ News publishing group in New Zealand, and had pioneered sales of its children's books into the US. One day, she was unceremoniously fired. At the age of 42, and after 22 years with the company, she was given five minutes to clear her desk and was then frog-marched out of the building. Although Wendy had never previously considered going out on her own, her reaction was swift and decisive. Within 24 hours, fuelled by a heavy dose of adversity and a desire for revenge, she decided to start a rival educational publishing business. She went on to become New Zealand's publishing queen and one of the country's most inspiring business success stories.

---

5. AN OPPORTUNITY BECKONS

The classic pull trigger is when you spot an opportunity – or when an opportunity spots you.

When you feel an opportunity beckoning you, something out there is pulling you off the ladder. You just know that this business opportunity has your name on it.

They say that 100 people can be looking at the same wall, but it is only the entrepreneur who sees a window of opportunity.

Take the case of Craig Smith, a professor of communication studies, who was invited in 1976 to deliver a guest lecture at the University of North Carolina. Since President Gerry Ford was addressing the Future Homemakers of America on the same campus, Craig went along – and was appalled when the president totally ignored the feminism issue.

Craig wrote to the White House, telling them what he thought of the President's performance.

A few days later, he was summoned to Washington. "If you can do better, show us," he was told.

Craig became Ford's longest serving speechwriter.

Case Study

Gary Klein was working for a New York shipper when he went to visit his dentist. As someone who kept several fish tanks at home, Gary noticed that the aquarium in the waiting room was in a deplorable state. He also knew exactly what needed to be done. Spotting a business opportunity, he offered to come and clean the dentist's aquarium each month for a small fee. Word spread and soon Gary had dozens of monthly clients. He advertised in local professional magazines, and was soon servicing hundreds of aquariums a month. He gave up his day job.

Many people start a business because their ideas have been rejected by their employers.

Rachael Lewis was a receptionist for an adult modelling agency in Miami. Looking for ways the agency could expand, she came up with the idea of developing a kids division. She took her plan to the owners of the agency, and offered to run the division.

When they rejected the idea, she left to found Rachael's Totz 'n' Teenz Model Management Inc., which she ran from her Manhattan apartment. Her agency went on to work with over 150 teen models, many of whom signed contracts with Ralph Lauren and Tommy Hilfiger.

Bernard Coyle used to return at the end of his bread delivery round with empty trays of crumbs. Customers would ask him for the breadcrumbs that gathered on the trays. So instead of throwing the breadcrumbs out, Bernard gave them to customers who used them as the base ingredient of stuffings for roasts and other dishes. Bernard suggested to his employer that this was an opportunity for an additional revenue stream.

When management displayed no interest in Bernard's idea, he left the business and set up his own dedicated award-winning breadcrumbs business, The Crumb Factory.

The thing to remember about triggers is that if you are already looking for an excuse to leave the ladder world, any trigger, push or pull, can be a healthy trigger.

And if you are not yet emotionally ready to switch gears to self-employment, any trigger, push or pull, can be the wrong trigger.

CHAPTER 6

What Do You Want To Be When You Grow Up?

You've reached the conclusion that you must leave the ladder world. You trust the triggers that push or pull you off the ladder.

But what business are you going to start?

Some people are fortunate enough to have always known what they want to do when they leave the ladder world.

But what if you have no idea what field to get into?

This was the dilemma I faced. My particular trigger was being fired from my last ladder job three days before I would have been made permanent.

After years of hopping from one ladder job to another, I knew that ladders were bad for my health. For the sake of my mental health, I knew I had to jump off the ladder permanently.

So I sat down at my kitchen table with a blank piece of paper in front of me. I drew 2 columns: one column was for the list of my skills, the second column was for the list of things that I really enjoyed doing.

This can't be difficult, I assured myself. But I was wrong. My MA had been in industrial sociology, but I had never worked as an industrial sociologist. I had managed departments and people, but were these real skills that I could build a business on?

I was used to following solicited and unsolicited advice from my elders and betters. I understood the language of 'I must.' I was unfamiliar with the language of 'I want'.

You can't start your own business unless you know what you want.

This was a moment of truth. It was time to look deep into my soul, and to ask myself what I really wanted to be when I grow up.

Back at my kitchen table, days turned into weeks. Weeks turned into three months. My family thought I was suffering from an early mid-life crisis. They could not understand why I refused to go and find another job. There were whispered discussions about bringing in the men in white coats. (More about family reactions in chapter 12.)

And then a chance encounter helped put the pieces of the entrepreneurial puzzle into place. A colleague asked me as a favour to write the text for a small brochure on a car alarm system he had developed. Without thinking too much about the fact that I had never before written a brochure, I wrote the text. For good measure, I even drew a rough sketch of the layout of the brochure.

A week later, the colleague called to tell me that his graphic designer wanted to meet me. "What's a graphic designer?" I asked. I knew nothing about the marketing or design industry. And somewhat suspiciously, I then asked: "And why does he want to meet me?"

"My graphic designer is the guy who is designing and producing my brochure," my friend explained patiently. "Based on the text you wrote for me, he wants to commission you to write texts for his other clients."

Bingo!

The penny dropped. I realised that I had chanced upon a niche market that uniquely suited my skills. Here was something I could do. Here was something I would love to do. I would become a copywriter – a word with which I was hitherto totally unfamiliar.

There was only one small problem. Becoming a copywriter meant being creative. Using my imagination. And in this area, I had a history. I had form, as they say in the sporting world.

Case Study

Before he left school, J received unsolicited career advice from two of his teachers. One teacher said to him, "You're a good B. So don't set your sights too high. Don't have ideas above your abilities. You are not A material, but you're also no dunce. There's no point applying to get into top colleges like Oxford or Cambridge University. Apply to a good solid regional university."

J thanked the teacher, and duly got a B grade in every subject in his final exams. He did not apply to Oxford or Cambridge. He was accepted by a regional university (in the first year after it achieved university status). He got a B grade in his BA.

The advice from the second teacher was equally well meaning, and equally misguided. "Whatever you do, don't write," she told J. "Thanks for the advice, Miss. May I ask why not?" "Because you lack imagination," she replied. J took her advice. After all, teachers know best. Not that J had ever had a burning desire to write, but thanks to the teacher's constructive advice, he did not put creative pen to paper for the next 10 years.

After completing two university degrees and floundering in a succession of dead-end ladder jobs, J decided to make a career out of writing. He went on to write a dozen books, became a newspaper columnist, a speechwriter and a blogger.

I can personally vouch for the veracity of this last case study. The J in this case study is me.

When I thought about it, I realised that bad advice notwithstanding, creativity had been a constant theme in my life. I used to enjoy sketching - boats, cars and landscapes. I used to perform puppet theatre shows. I used to write scripts for school revues. I used to act in school plays. I used to build cardboard models, then plastic models. The week Ashi was born, I bought him a huge Lego set, and spent the next few years practicing until he was old enough to enjoy it.

More bits of the puzzle fell into place. I had a life-long fascination with words. I'd been an avid Scrabble player since I was 8. I loved puns. I loved word games. I had always devoured anything in print, from the small print on the cereal packet to the ads in the paper. So here was a way of matching my language skills, my creativity and my love of words.

Based on the swiftest and most shallow exercise in market research in entrepreneurial history, I decided that there was a niche for freelance copywriting: writing advertising, marketing and promotional texts. After all, I already had one client, my friend's graphic designer.

How hard could it be to find more clients who appreciated my skills? I bought myself a second-hand electric typewriter (this was in the dark ages before the PC), I created a company name, I bought myself some Letraset (remember what that is?) to create a logo, and had business cards printed. Driven by a magnificent mix of naivety and confidence, I found myself in business.

Almost 15 years after leaving school, I had finally discovered what I wanted to be when I grew up. And although over the ensuing years I have greatly expanded the repertoire of my business offering, I still write brochures, websites, speeches and presentations for clients all over the world.

And I still love it.

I sometimes wonder whether the people who dish out career advice so liberally realise just what an awesome responsibility they carry. Misguided negative feedback can dent our self-confidence, undermine our self-image, and shatter our dreams.

Luckily, not every student listens to bad advice. Kentucky high school student Patricia Galloway was a dancer, a member of the drama club, and an artist. While attending an obligatory lecture by a professor of engineering who had brought along several renderings of buildings, she heard him say that women had great opportunities in engineering.

Patricia was hooked, and on the spot, she decided to become a civil engineer. Her career guidance counsellor said: "Bad idea. Your aptitude test scores do not indicate a career in engineering." And even when she was accepted to Purdue University's school of engineering, a professor told her she shouldn't be there. "Women should not be in engineering."

She graduated with a degree in civil engineering, became CEO and Principal of the Nielsen-Wurster Group, an international management consulting company, and ended up being elected the first woman ever to serve as president of the American Society of Civil Engineers.

When Sir Anthony Sher was a young unknown actor freshly arrived in London from his native South Africa, he managed to get an audition at Rada, the Royal Academy of Dramatic Arts. Some weeks after the audition, he received a letter informing him that he had failed his audition for a place in this prestigious drama school.

The writer of the rejection letter chose to share some advice with Sher: "Not only have you failed, and you must not try again, but we most seriously urge you to think of a different career."

Fortunately for us, Sher ignored this advice, and went on to become one of the most gifted actors of his generation.

Albert Einstein's father was told by his high school teacher: "It doesn't matter what he does – he will never amount to anything." Einstein was later refused a place at the Munich Technical Institute because he "showed no promise."

John Warnock, the engineer who helped found Adobe Systems Inc., was told by a school counsellor: "Your probability of having any kind of success in any engineering-related activity is probably zero."

Don't ever let somebody tell you you can't do something. You got a dream - you gotta protect it. When people can't do somethin' themselves, they wanna tell you you can't do it.
Will Smith in the movie Happyness

Some of us receive genuinely valuable advice. In later years, we look back in gratitude to the adult who helped steer us in a positive direction. And even if we do not act upon this advice, we are thankful for it. Others among us do not want advice. We don't listen to advice, and we don't follow advice.

But many of us belong to the third category - we receive bad advice and believe it!

Whatever category you belong to, in the end you must find your own route to the magic moment of truth.

Some people have always known what they wanted to do when they grow up.

Some people only discover their route when they are already on the ladder.

And some people must first jump off the ladder before they find their route.

CHAPTER 7
Self-belief and other prerequisites for being your own boss

Do you need special personality or character traits to decide to become your own boss?

Opinions differ. Some people claim that there is no such thing as a definable predisposition to entrepreneurship.

We can't lump all entrepreneurs together. There's a danger that lists of entrepreneurial qualities can end up sounding like horoscopes or self-assessment tests. But I do believe that you need a healthy mix of specific traits if you're going to get off the ladder and go it alone.

Psychologist John D Gartner suggests 10 entrepreneurial attributes:

1 Grand ambitions	6 Risk-taking
2 Energy	7 Impulsiveness
3 Ideas	8 Fast-talking
4 Restlessness	9 Wittiness
5 Euphoria	10 Irritation at obstacles

Jim Rohn lists 10 qualities more valuable than start-up capital:

1 Ambition	6 Faith
2 Time	7 Ingenuity
3 Desperation	8 Heart and Soul
4 Determination	9 Personality
5 Courage	10 Charisma

Ryan P. M. Allis, author of *From Zero to One Million*, asked successful entrepreneurs to rank 15 entrepreneurial qualities:

1 Being able to build a solid team	8 Being able to execute
2 Leadership and the ability to inspire	9 Having a bias toward action
3 Persistence	10 Having a good idea or plan
4 Motivation and ambition	11 Knowledge of marketing
5 Integrity	12 Good networking skills
6 Ability to communicate effectively	13 Having the right advisors
	14 Knowledge of accounting and finance
7 Confidence	15 A college degree

I find it fascinating and amusing that knowledge of accounting and having a college degree came last!

Multi-billionaire Oracle founder Larry Ellison claims that his entrepreneurial success is due to constantly questioning conventional wisdom, doubting the experts, and questioning authority.

Here is my own list of entrepreneurial qualities:

1   SELF-BELIEF

Anyone starting a business needs a healthy quotient of self-confidence, self-esteem and self-belief. If your business venture is going to succeed, you must believe in yourself. If you agonise over every decision, and constantly worry about whether you did the right thing, you may never get your business off the ground.

> *"If people believe in themselves,*
> *it's amazing what they can accomplish."*
> Sam Walton

People who believe in themselves also believe that nothing is impossible. They know that they are capable of accomplishing anything they set their mind to, and they do not accept that just because something has not been done before, it's not worth trying.

Confidence is not measured in decibels. Being confident is not the same as being an extrovert.

Although I freely admit that I am an extrovert and that my decibel level is high, I know plenty of people who express their confidence in a much quieter manner.

And that's fine too.

> *"When you have confidence, you can have a lot of fun.*
> *And when you have fun, you can do amazing things."*
> Joe Namath

2   STUBBORNNESS

One thing about the entrepreneurial experience is guaranteed: there will be plenty of surprises and obstacles along the way. Goal posts will move, people will let you down, and unexpected scenarios will disturb your plans.

Which is why you need to be so single-minded and focussed. You can't afford to be sidetracked. When you believe in something, keep at it. Be stubborn in the pursuit of your goals. Stay disciplined and focused.

We use many different words to describe the kind of single-mindedness you need as an entrepreneur: Determination, Persistence, Tenacity, Steadfastness, Doggedness, Stubbornness, Perseverance, Pig-headedness, Resoluteness, Decisiveness and Discipline.

You need a good mix of all of these.

Shortly after Marianne Gunn O'Connor's fashion business in Dublin went into liquidation, she was asked to read the manuscript of a novel. She liked it, and tried to get it published. She contacted Peter Straus at Picador, who agreed to read the manuscript. But Marianne stubbornly refused to hand it over unless she could do so in person. Straus agreed to meet her the day before he was due to fly to America. Again Marianne refused, insisting that the hand-over take place on the morning of Straus' flight. So they met for an early morning breakfast in Dublin Airport. As Marianne explained later, "I had to make sure he had the manuscript on the flight. The chances of him actually reading the manuscript were higher if he was stuck in an aircraft above the Atlantic." Her stubbornness paid off. As soon as Straus arrived in New York, he faxed her: "Don't go anywhere else with this, I'm buying it." Marianne later pulled off a literary coup when she secured the million-dollar deal for Irish Prime Minister Bertie Ahern's 21-year-old daughter Cecilia for her first novel PS I love You.

Entrepreneurial experts claim that too many people give up just before they would have made a breakthrough. They stop wooing a client just before they would have landed a big order. They stop developing a new idea just before it would have been snapped up in the marketplace.

There is a story circulating in my family about giving up too early. According to family legend, Joseph Fachler, whose Turkish passport had saved him during WW2, was trying to augment his income in post-war Brussels, Belgium, by making hand-made chocolates in his basement. He sold the chocolates through local shops, but at a certain point he decided that there was no future in chocolates. He sold his chocolate-making machinery, and sought his fame and fortune in other fields.

In the same street in Brussels, chocolatier Joseph Draps was rebuilding his chocolate company founded before the war. He saw a future in chocolates, and stubbornly worked on his chocolate range named after the legendary Lady Godiva. The first Godiva shop outside Belgium was opened in Paris in 1958. In 1966, Godiva reached the USA, became part of the Campbell Soups company, and was purchased by a Turkish company in 2008 for $850 million.

So you can understand why every time I see Godiva chocolates piled high in an airport duty-free shop, I imagine what would have happened if the other Joseph had hung in there.

I'd be seeing Fachler chocolates piled high in every airport!

Case Study

Milena Zilo failed in her attempt to get accepted into the University of Denver's highly regarded finance programme. She was so devastated that she hid the letter from her parents. But she picked herself up, and walked into the office of the vice chancellor of enrolment, John Dolan, loudly announcing that she would not leave until Dolan admitted her to the school. Dolan's secretary successfully protected her boss, so Milena grabbed a promotional brochure that featured Dolan's photo, and walked around the campus until she tracked him down. "There's been a mistake. All I want is 5 minutes of your time," she said. He agreed to listen to her story. After examining her notebook of recommendations and achievements, he acknowledged that a mistake had indeed been made, and offered her a scholarship.

---

3   IMAGINATION

"Imagination is more important than knowledge."
Albert Einstein

You probably would never have thought of starting your own business unless you were inquisitive and curious.

You must keep an eye out for anything that could affect your business. You must keep up to date with new ideas, new methods and new trends. You must know what the competition is doing and planning. You must look out for innovative ways of doing things.

If you can imagine and visualise your business and how it will run, you will find it much easier to fill in the dots.

Visualisation helps to bring your entrepreneurial dream to life. If you can get excited about what you visualise, this excitement will spur you on to turn it into reality.

4   PIGEONS AND STATUES

> *"The only thing that makes life possible is*
> *permanent, intolerable uncertainty."*
> Ursula K. LeGuin

Running a business is a roller-coaster experience. One day we're up, one day we're down. One day we're on top of the world, feeling in control. We are flying merrily around like a pigeon, looking for a statue on which to perch, and on which we can drop what pigeons drop on statues. Another day, we're a statue, just standing there while pigeons perch on us and do their business. One day we feel that nothing can stop us, one day we feel that nothing is going right.

The pigeon and statue concept was first introduced to me by Alan Clark. Whenever we chat on the phone, exchange emails or meet in person, the first question is always: "Are you having a pigeon day or a statue day?"

There is no mistaking a pigeon day. Even if we have been on our feet all day long, we are oozing energy. There is also no mistaking a statue day. Even if we have been sitting on our backside all day long, we are drained of energy.

On a pigeon day, we feel vindicated and validated. We know that we made the right decision to take the entrepreneurial plunge. On a statue day, we feel despondent and frustrated. We are no longer so convinced about the wisdom of forsaking the security of the ladder world.

On a pigeon day, we take everything in our stride. On a statue day, we ask ourselves why all the pigeons in the business world have chosen today to visit us. We feel burnt-out. We have no enthusiasm for our work. Everything bothers us. We lose our perspective. We feel we can't trust anyone's judgement. We question the value of our work.

On a pigeon day, no one can insult us, no one gets on our nerves, no one can take the smile off our face. We feel vital and energetic.

On a statue day, no amount of extra sleep or vitamin boosts will help us feel better disposed to fellow members of the human race. Anyone and everyone manages to zap our energy. Our customers drain our energy with their incessant demand for attention and service. Our suppliers drain our energy with their demands for payment. Our bank drains our energy with its demand that we cover the overdraft. Our staff drains our energy with their demands for more pay. And our family drains our energy with its demands for more attention.

Statue days are part of the entrepreneurial equation. They are an inevitable consequence of trying to cope with the pressure of starting and operating a business. And I have yet to meet an entrepreneur who has never ever succumbed to statue day blues.

The US Small Business Administration (SBA) itemises the main reasons why 60% of small businesses fold within the first six years: They grow too fast; they have a non-viable concept; they are not good at marketing or sales; they fail to plan; they start without enough money to reach breakeven; and they lack control of their finances and books.

But what these statistics don't tell us is how many new businesses fold because their owners' statue days outweigh their pigeon days. The figures do not tell us how many business owners give up because they have run out of motivational steam.

Despite (or maybe because of) nearly 3 decades of running my own business, I am not immune to statue day blues. And I too need a constant flow of motivational fuel.

The entrepreneurial roller-coaster means being able to live with uncertainty. People who need a high level of predictability in their lives rarely risk the uncertainty of starting their own business. But entrepreneurs thrive in an unstructured environment.

Situations that can send shivers down the spines of ladder people also send shivers down the spines of entrepreneurs - except that these are not shivers of fear, they are tingles of excitement!

> *Entrepreneurship finds many, but only the brave find entrepreneurship.*
> Suzanne Mulvehill

Entrepreneurs are often stereotyped as risk-takers. Personally, I don't think that risk-taking distinguishes ladder people from entrepreneurs. What's different is the definition of risk.

For many entrepreneurs, starting a business in a field that no one else has tried is the result of original and creative thinking, not of risk-taking.

Many entrepreneurs would define their actions as survival, not as risk. Just because every new business venture contains an element of risk doesn't make you a risk freak. From the outside looking in, starting your own business can look risky when compared to the so-called security of working for someone else. From the inside looking out, it feels like something that you simply have to do if you want to follow your own star.

"If you don't risk anything you risk even more.
Erica Jong

You must learn to thrive in the pigeon and statue world. There is never a guarantee that the products or services that you offer now will still be in demand in six months time. A major client may drop you. You have to learn to think on your feet, remain flexible, and not to be thrown by every change of plan.

Talking of pigeons, here's a parable:

It was a cold winter's night, and the little pigeon could not find any warm shelter. As it flew around, it got colder and colder, until its little wings froze solid and it fell to the ground. It lay there freezing, certain that death was just moments away. Suddenly, the little pigeon felt a warm sensation. As it hovered back to consciousness, it realised that a friendly cow had dropped a luxurious deposit all over it. The warmth gave the little pigeon a new lease of life, and it started cooing for joy. A passing fox heard the cooing, located the heap, carefully removed the excrement, and promptly devoured the little pigeon.

There are three entrepreneurial lessons that we can learn from this parable:

1. *If someone shits on you, they are not necessarily your enemy.*

2. *If someone gets you out of the shit, they are not necessarily your friend.*

3. *If you are in the shit and happy, keep your mouth shut.*

5   ENERGY

Entrepreneurs believe that they are capable of accomplishing anything they want. You can almost see the energy bursting out of

them. Entrepreneurs are also highly motivated and always enthusiastic. Where others see disaster, they see potential.

People will tell you that unless you are prepared to work hard, you should not start a company.

I beg to disagree.

Unless you already work hard, don't even think of starting your own business.

Atari founder Nolan Bushnell said that it all comes down to one critical ingredient: "Getting off your ass and doing something."

A high energy level is a must if you are starting your own business. You will need to be prepared to put in a constant and consistent effort, and devote long hours to your business. If you are a morning person, don't get into a business that requires staying up late. If you're a night person, you won't be too happy running an early morning delivery business.

You need to give your business 100 percent. Your customers need to know that you are devoting 100 percent of your time and focus to their needs.

6   PASSSION

"We may affirm absolutely that nothing great in the world has been accomplished without passion."
Hegel

There is nothing quite like the pride, the passion and the sense of ownership you experience when you have your own business. It is wonderful to be engaged in something that you can be truly proud of, knowing that it's yours, that you created it, that you're responsible for its success.

It's like having a child, and you will find that owning your business defines you. You will experience the special thrill of providing a service or manufacturing a product that people want.

You have to be passionate about your new business. You must feel a burning desire to nurture your business, commit to it, and passionately work for its success.

The Mountain

There were two tribes in the Andes. One tribe lived in a village in the lowlands, at the foot of the mountain, and the other tribe lived in a village high in the mountains. One day, a raiding party of mountain people invaded the lowlanders. They kidnapped a lowlander baby and took the infant with them back up into the mountains.

The lowlanders didn't know how to climb the mountain. They didn't know any of the trails that the mountain people used. They didn't know where to find the mountain people or how to track them in the steep terrain.

Nevertheless, the lowlanders sent out a party of their strongest men to climb the mountain and bring the baby home. The men tried first one method of climbing and then another. They tried one trail and then another. But after several days of effort, they had only climbed a few hundred feet.

Feeling hopeless, the lowlanders decided that there was no point continuing, and they prepared to return to their village below.

As they were packing their gear for the descent, they saw a figure emerging from the mist. Then they saw that it was the baby's mother walking toward them.

She was coming down the mountain - and here they were, unable to figure out how to climb up any further.

The lowlanders then noticed that she had the baby strapped to her back. In amazement, they asked her: "How were you able to climb this mountain when we, the strongest and most able men in the village, could not?"
She shrugged her shoulders and said:

"It wasn't your baby."

7   CRAZINESS

120 pairs of eyes were focused on the speaker as he energetically walked up to the podium. We had all joined a 2-year programme for entrepreneurs. This was the opening address on the opening day of the programme. We were anxious to hear from our guest speaker, serial entrepreneur John Teeling.

He looked at us and said: "I understand that everyone here runs their own business." Pause. "Are you mad?" he roared.

We were shocked. Had we come here to be insulted? "You must be crazy," he continued. "Anyone who leaves the security of the corporate world to open their own business must be mad."

For the next half an hour, John Teeling made us laugh with his stories of the problems he had with bankers, lawyers, government officials, and others who had tried to stop him from realising his dream.

Accept the crazy label. Accept that anyone with an entrepreneurial mindset needs to be MAD.

- the **M**eans (capital, access to resources)
- the **A**bility (physical/mental capacity to marshal resources)
- the **D**esire to materialize their vision.

"You're only given a little spark of madness. You mustn't lose it."
Robin Williams

You need to be a little crazy to leave the safe haven of the corporate world and open your own business.

You have to be off-the-wall to face of the frightening statistics that for every 100 entrepreneurs who opened their new business yesterday, over half will have gone out of business within the next three years.

When you embark on the entrepreneurial journey, it should feel like fun. You are allowed to enjoy yourself. You are allowed to give your impish sense of humour an opportunity to express itself. Go on, I give you permission.

Case Study

Richard Branson never missed an opportunity to get a swipe at British Airways. To celebrate the introduction of Virgin's first Airbus A340-600, which was at the time the world's longest airliner, he emblazoned on the fuselage for everyone in Heathrow to see the unforgettable slogan: 'Mine's Bigger Than Yours'.

"If at first an idea is not absurd, it has no hope."
Albert Einstein

8   RESOURCEFULNESS

Entrepreneurs are doers, not observers. They are quick to take the initiative and are quick to recognise and seize opportunities. They are proactive, and cannot stand procrastination. They want to get on with things.

Your primary responsibility as a business owner is to find the most effective ways of bringing your business to the notice of your potential clients. There is no room for shyness. You need to be upfront, upbeat and resourceful about your business, your products and your services.

"Don't just stand there, make it happen."
Lee Iacocca

Don't sit and wait for things to happen – because they won't. "If it's to be, it's up to me," should be your mantra. Initiative is a daily, even an hourly, imperative.

Steve Latour was trying to persuade the 1-800-FLOWERS national flower company to handle his handmade Hawaiian leis. He knew that senior 1-800-FLOWERS executives were meeting in their Long Island offices, and he wanted to come up with something that would catch their attention.

He hired an actor and hired a gorilla suit, as well as a white tuxedo and top hat. The smartly-dressed gorilla arrived at the 1-800-FLOWERS HQ and handed out Hawaiian-style pizzas to all the executives. They chuckled at Steve's gesture, and rewarded him with the contract to supply them with his handmade Hawaiian leis.

Here is another resourcefulness stories involving an actor. Yossi Abramowitz sought funding for his family-oriented ezine targeted at the family market. His business angel target was the CEO of a major law firm. All his attempts by smail mail, email and FedEx to get past the gatekeepers failed.

So Abramowitz hired an actor, dressed him in a Barney the Dinosaur costume, placed a bouquet of balloons in one hand and the business plan in the other, and deposited him outside the CEO's head office. The security guard waved him in, and everywhere Barney went, his fans greeted him with laughter. When he reached the executive floor, his way was blocked by a stern-looking receptionist whose job it was to ensure that only people with an appointment got past. She threw her arms around Barney's neck. "Barney! I read your comics. I have Barney dolls. I watch you on TV. What can I do for you?" And thus it was that Barney made his way unimpeded to the desk of the CEO's personal assistant, handed her the balloons, and gave her the precious business plan.

Resourcefulness is needed when you want to build your new business and you have no marketing budget. Here is how various entrepreneurs generated publicity for their ventures:

Each week, Gary Hirshberg of Stonyfield Farm delivered his natural yogurt to delis in the Boston region. One morning, he heard a radio talk-show host boast: "I would rather eat camel dung than natural food." The next day, Hirschberg turned up at the radio station with a pail of his organic yogurt, and a pail of frozen camel dung. The staff went live with the story, which was picked up by thousands of other radio stations. Stonyfield is now the largest natural yogurt company in the USA.

Barry Potekin opened his first Gold Coast Dogs restaurant as an upscale fast-food operation in Chicago, but had no money left for advertising. Each morning, he randomly hailed a cab outside the restaurant, asked the driver to drive round the block, and told the driver why he should eat at Gold Coast Dogs. Potekin paid his fare, and gave the driver a free lunch voucher. Before long, cabbies were double parking outside Gold Coast Dogs.

When Simon Woodroffe (of Dragon's Den fame) was opening his new Yo! Sushi restaurant in London, he wanted to create the impression that he had prestigious multinational backers. He asked Japanese auto and bike maker Honda for funds. They refused, but agreed to loan him a motorbike. He also persuaded All Nippon Airways to upgrade him when he flew to Japan to conduct his research. He then wrote to the two companies that as an expression of his gratitude, he was appointing them official sponsors. When he did not receive any communication turning down his offer, Woodroffe displayed the Honda and All Nippon logos prominently on the menus, on the window, and on the delivery bikes. Suddenly, investors and banks were taking note of the new sushi restaurant with the famous backers.

If you check the backgrounds of many people who chose the entrepreneurial route, you will discover that they displayed resourcefulness in earning extra pocket money while they were growing up. Not only because they want the extra dough, but because moneymaking opportunities came along - and they seized the initiative.

At boarding school, I used to earn extra money by typing class work for my classmates, and by shining shoes for lazy sixth formers. At University, I ran a small grocery supply company to help pay my tuition. (Strangely, at the time, I did not define this as an entrepreneurial activity.)

CHAPTER 8
Entrepreneurs and Ladder People – worlds apart

I remember an incident halfway through my ladder career that illustrates why I believe that ladder people and entrepreneurs are totally different breeds. I had gone to my dad to ask his advice about moving from one ladder to another. His response puzzled me:

"What are the chances of you taking over the company you work in at present?"

At the time, I felt that this was a very strange question. And what did it have to do with my question?

I did not understand that my dad was speaking non-ladder talk. In his entrepreneurial world, it was logical that everyone should want to own their own company. In his world, if you cannot become the boss, move to a company where you can. His advice was based on his strong entrepreneurial values.

I had asked him a question in ladder-speak, he had answered in entrepreneur-speak.

As I said earlier, I make no claim for the superiority of the ladder world or the non-ladder world. Neither breed is superior. But if you are planning to move from the ladder to the entrepreneurial world, you need to be aware of the conceptual and perceptual chasm that divides the two worlds. The very things that turn an entrepreneur on, can have the opposite effect on ladder people. The two worlds are often on a collision course.

The ladder world can view the entrepreneurial world with suspicion, incomprehension and hostility. Envy might be one cause. Maybe ladder people feel that entrepreneurs are more vital, more alive, more creative.

The ladder world gives many people a sense of security. They like the fact that their work life is organised and structured.

Entrepreneurs look to themselves to provide security. Naturally, they miss the regular salary, but they are worried that they will pay too high a price by living in the salary world.

Specifically, there is a very different attitude to time and pace in the two worlds. The people inhabiting these worlds wear different watches.

Even the most dedicated salaried employee fits their time input to corporate demands. Employees work for specified periods in a specified location. They focus their time and efforts on accomplishing work assignments without being encumbered by the demands at home.

But as an entrepreneur, you have no one to tell you where and when to work. There is a thinner line between home and work, and demands between the two can overlap. Time management is self-driven. You're the one who dictates the day's schedule. You make the clock fit your schedule.

Imagine that during the course of a working day in your ladder job, you look at your watch (we're talking about the old-fashioned clock-face, not digital.) What do you see?

Well, I'll tell you what you don't see. You don't see a clock-face with 12 equidistant numerals. Any time a ladder person looks at their watch while at work, what they see is always in relation to the distance between 9 and 5.

On the ladder, we never look at the time in neutral mode. We never say to ourselves: "Oh, how interesting, the time is 10.44 am." The time that we see on our watch is always relative to how much time has elapsed since we arrived at work, and how long before the next coffee break, lunch break, or clocking out time.

If it is indeed 10.44, you probably make a mental note that it's 16 minutes to the 11.00 coffee break. If it's 12.44, you know it's soon time for lunch. If it's 16.44, you are already on a countdown to clocking out. If it's after 18.00, you are wondering why you're not home yet - or you're busy calculating your overtime pay.

Now let's consider the clock-face on the entrepreneur's watch. When you work for yourself, time has a very different value. Time is the enemy, because you are always trying to squeeze more than 24 hours into your day. When you look at your watch, you don't see 12 equidistant numerals. What you see is a jumble of deadlines, a queue of competing priorities waiting to be attended to.

There is always something else that should have been completed by now. An urgent call to your customer. Placing an urgent order with a supplier. Lodging money in the bank. Chasing up money you are owed.

In short, **when you run your own business, it is always the wrong time!**

Entrepreneurs need to establish a flexible relationship with coffee breaks and meals. When you make the switch from employee to self-employed, you need to leave your old watch behind in your place of work, and buy a new watch for your entrepreneurial adventure.

It's not just in the workplace that the differences between the two worlds are apparent. It happens in the home as well. Ladder folk can have a real problem understanding how you can be at work if you're at home. They are not comfortable with unnatural entrepreneurial work practices. For them, home is not for work. If you're home, it means you've got time to run errands, do the shopping, and fix the plastering that fell off the wall.

Entrepreneurs can have a hard time convincing their ladder partners that when they are sitting at home looking as if they are doing nothing, they could be planning staffing rosters, debating whether to invest in a new cellphone, or trying to come up with a new promotional strapline.

Some years ago, a client for whom I had conducted a major rewrite of their online help desk, asked me to spend a couple of days in their head office. I was given a desk and a computer, and was available to troubleshoot in real time as the development team put the finishing touches to the project.

I suffered genuine culture shock. It had been years since I had sat a full day in an office, and I had forgotten what office life can be like.

This was a hard working, smart and committed team, but I was taken aback by their work ethic. I could not believe the eagerness with which they awaited lunch, the amount of time devoted to discussing where they were going to have lunch, the length of time they actually spent at lunch, and the extra time spent at lunch when they knew that their supervisor was not in the office.

I'm not saying this was wrong.

It was a sharp reminder of the very different work environments, work ethics and work norms in the ladder and non-ladder worlds.

CHAPTER 9
7 fun things about being your own boss

"It is our choices, Harry, that show what we truly are, far more than our ambitions."
Professor Dumbledore to Harry Potter

If I had to encapsulate the benefits of working for yourself in 3 words, I would say "Freedom to choose."

Being an entrepreneur is all about freedom and autonomy. The freedom to use all you talents, to follow your own initiatives, to pursue your own ideas, to rely on your own imagination, and to change direction whenever you want. All the benefits described in this chapter revolve around this theme.

1   YOU DICTATE YOUR PRIORITIES

In the ladder world, you probably encountered plenty of examples of inept decision making. Are they blind? you asked yourself about your bosses. Can't they see where this will lead?

Now, at last, it's your turn. Making decisions about everything can be very empowering. The premises. The staffing. The equipment. The layout. The name of the company. The website. Everything. It's yours. You get to put your personal stamp on absolutely everything. And it can be a very exhilarating experience.

You're the one who dictates the priorities. You call the shots. There is no longer anyone else telling you what to do and when to do it. You're the one who has to balance the competing demands of clients, suppliers, the bank and other stakeholders.

2   YOU CHOOSE WHOM TO WORK WITH

You may choose to work entirely on your own, answering to a variety of descriptions: Soloist, Freelancer, Solo operator, Sole trader, Sole proprietor, Consultant, Contractor or Lone wolf.

You may not necessarily be interested in empire building. You may be more interested in building a career than equity. But you can be driven by the same sense of energy, excitement, enthusiasm and motivation as entrepreneurs who go on to create much larger businesses.

If you choose to take on staff, you will no longer be stuck with other people's decisions. You can choose people who brighten up the day, not people who cast a shadow over it. You can scrupulously choose people who are on your side, who share your vision for your business. You no longer have to accept the ineptitude of a colleague whom you would never have hired. You no longer have to work alongside a nasty colleague. And you no longer have to accept the whims of a bullying boss.

The same goes for clients and suppliers. You no longer have to put up with a rude and arrogant client, or an unpleasant or unreliable supplier.

You can decide to choose a different model of employer/employee relationships. If you want to use ethical criteria in choosing staff, clients or suppliers, you won't be the first. JC Penney called his first retail outlets *Golden Rule Stores*, because he insisted that his employees never touched alcohol or tobacco!

Another option is to choose to go into business with a partner – always bearing in mind that partnerships can be fraught if you choose the wrong person.

In my business career, I have tried all three options. I started out on my own. I then tried hiring staff. I then went back to being on my own. And recently, for the first time, I went into partnership in one of my business interests. I always got on well with Ron Immink, from the time we met when he worked at Oak Tree Press, my original publisher. Our work overlapped frequently when Ron worked in invent, the DCU Innovation and Enterprise Centre. So when I wanted to develop my book-based executive development methodology, I invited Ron to be my partner in Bookbuzz.

3   YOU CHOOSE WHERE YOU WORK

You get to decide where you work. You choose whether to buy or rent your own premises. You choose whether you want to work closer to home. You choose whether you want to work from home.

Some people regard running a business from home as a short-term solution while they search for suitable premises. Others see it as a permanent solution. Advantages to working from home include no more rush-hour commute, no boss breathing down your neck, more work / family flexibility, and cost savings.

Based on your needs, you might work from your basement, attic, garage, under the staircase, garden shed, mobile home in the garden, living room, kitchen table, or converted bedroom.

Over the years, I have tried several combinations. When I first started out as a freelance copywriter, having my own office outside the home with its own address felt more like a real business.

Some years later, when I no longer employed staff, I decided to try living and working in the same place. Most people who make this decision convert part of their home into an office space. I did the opposite. I built a loft above my desk, and for years I lived in my workspace instead of working in my living space. I enjoyed the arrangement, but my sons (who had already left home) thought it was strange that their father lived in a tree house.

For the last few years, for the first time, I have been working in a dedicated office space in my home, and it's great. (Of course, it takes a special type of spouse to put up with the special type of disarray this can introduce into a home.)

The real question about running a business from home is whether you are temperamentally suited to do so. Do you have the self-discipline to work from home? Will you be able to motivate yourself to sit down and work on whatever needs to be done? Can you withstand the distractions? You will have to educate your family – partner, kids, parents, pets - that when you are working in your business space, you are off-limits.

Some businesses are more suited to being home-based than others. Here's a partial list:

Accountant	Marketing consultant
Alternative medical practitioner	Painter
Architect	Masseur/masseuse
Artist	Photographer
Beautician	Physician
Business consultant	Physiotherapist
Computer repair	Plumber
Copywriter	PR consultant
Corporate trainer	Programmer
Event management	Property consultant
Freelance office services	Psychotherapist
Graphic designer	Surveyor
Hairdresser	Telemarketing
Health and fitness professional	Virtual PA
Interior designer	Web designer
Journalist	Writer/editor

In order to combat cabin fever, try scheduling appointments in a neutral venue (hotel lobby, coffee shop) as a way of getting you out your home. Take a break from the routine. Do some stretching exercises, take a walk around the block.

4   YOU'RE ALLOWED TO DO NOTHING

There are very few ladder jobs where you can sit at your desk and be seen to be doing nothing. It doesn't look right and it doesn't feel right. In the ladder world, looking busy is equated with good performance.

As your own boss, you are allowed to give your mind a little break after completing a project, landing a big job, or receiving fantastic accolades from your client.

It is perfectly legitimate to do absolutely nothing! No more having to look as if you're busy. No more having to impress anyone.

Sit there and do nothing for as long as you like.

Obviously, I don't recommend this as a permanent state of mind, but now that you're in charge, you are allowed to make the most of it.

5   YOU CAN PLAY HOOKY

Just imagine the look of puzzlement on your supervisor's face in a ladder job if you announced in the middle of the afternoon that you are popping out to choose a wedding anniversary card for your spouse. It's just not done, is it?

But when you have your own business, you can decide your schedule. You can work when there is work to be done, and you can take off whenever you feel like it - even if the work isn't finished. It's your decision. You decide the priorities. If you want to take time off, you don't have to call in sick. You don't have to feel guilty.

"Every now and then, go away, have a little relaxation. For when you come back to your work, your judgement will be surer."
Leonardo da Vinci

The only person you owe any explanation to is yourself - and if you're smart, you'll go easy on yourself. Feel like a stroll in the park? Just do it. A lunchtime concert? No problem. A siesta because you worked late into the night? That's your privilege. You can go shopping, go to a museum, or attend a course or lecture.

Feel like pampering yourself? Go and get a facial. Get your hair done. Go to the gym. Find another entrepreneur to play squash with in the middle of the day. And if you work entirely by yourself, you can even decide not to go in to the office at all today.

Being your own boss also means that you can take your vacations out of season, when there are less crowds and less of a hole in your pocket.

Case Study

Judith ran an Ecommerce site that specialised in holiday gift packages. Her busiest season was in the run-up to Christmas and the New Year. She and her staff would work round the clock to fill orders, and she would arrive at the Christmas table in an advanced state of stress. Her children, her spouse and her parents all suffered. One year, Judith informed her family and friends that she was postponing Christmas, which they would all celebrate on the 15th of January. She booked a hotel (paying low off-peak rates) for the weekend, and organised a party for family and friends. Judith enjoyed a stress-free and guilt-free vacation, and spent more quality time with her family than ever before.

You don't need to ask permission for time off to attend a wedding or a funeral. You don't owe any explanation to anyone. Take the day off. Do something totally non-work related.

6   YOU DICTATE YOUR OWN SCHEDULE

As an entrepreneur, you decide how to fill your schedule. Being your own boss allows you to invest time and thought to nonbusiness activities. You decide how many hours you're going to spend on what. You decide how much time to devote to your family, to your interests, to your extra-curricular activities.

Shortly after I started my first business, I joined my local drama group, and discovered an acting talent that I did not know I had. Although I enjoyed the acting, I became more interested in the organisational side of things.

So I took over the drama group's publicity. I opened a dialogue with other "rival" drama groups. I organised a national festival, which turned into an annual event. I wrote and edited a national newsletter. I founded a national association of drama groups, and even joined the executive board of the International Amateur Theatre Association.

The point about all this unpaid activity, which I conducted from my desk, is that this was my own choice. I had to balance my paid work and my theatre work. And there is no doubt that over the years, the contacts I made in the world of international theatre certainly helped my business.

And the fact that today my repertoire of services includes presentation skills is directly linked to my acting background. I would never have gained the experience and expertise to coach CEOs, politicians and public figures in public speaking without all those years running drama workshops.

7 YOU CAN HAVE FUN

Being your own boss should – nay, must – also be fun. Be creative in finding ways of stimulating your fun gene.

I like to nurture my imagination by keeping special objects in my workspace - both as an inspiration and as a reminder not to take myself too seriously.

Pride of place goes to Figment, mascot of the Kodak Pavilion of Imagination, in Disneyworld's Epcot Center in Florida. I was greatly inspired there when I visited some 25 years ago. Ever since, everything I have written has been under the watchful eye of Figment as he sits on the shelf opposite me.

Certificate of the Right to Play
devised by Bruce Williamson

By this Certificate, know ye that *(insert your own name)* is a lifetime member and in good standing in the Society of Childlike Grownups and is hereby and forever entitled to walk in the rain, smell flowers, blow bubbles, splash in mud puddles, howl at the moon, and do anything else that brings more harmony, peace, and life energy to the above named member and to other humans and beings on this planet. Furthermore, the above named member is officially authorized to frequent all mountain tops, meadows, amusement parks, and the many other places where children of all ages come to play, and is encouraged to always remember the motto of the Society of Childlike Grownups: "You're never too old for recess."

---

8   YOU CAN'T BE FIRED!

Never again will you have to suffer the indignity and insult of hearing those dreaded words made famous by Donald Trump and Sir Alan Sugar in the US and UK versions of the TV show, The Apprentice: "You're fired."

CHAPTER 10
Bad things can happen to nice entrepreneurs

Moving off the ladder to start your own business can give you a great buzz. Once you make your decision, you will thrive on the excitement. You are borne on a wave of enthusiasm so intense that you are ready to face anything.

But there can be problems too. From every direction. And it's better to know about them in advance.

In the run-up to opening your new venture, you will be busy getting everything in place for the launch date. But once the business is up and running, problems will emerge. Some of these problems can be classified as business problems. Others are more emotional.

Let's look at the business problems first.

BAD THING 1: DOUBTERS AND BEGRUDGERS

While your decision to become an entrepreneur will elicit intense admiration in some circles, it will also elicit envy, resentment, jealousy and anger.

There will be no shortage of people who cast doubt on your business dream. Potential customers who don't appreciate your brilliance. Suppliers who don't believe you are credit worthy. Banks who laugh at your application for a start-up loan.

In the face of all these, you will have to develop a thick skin.

The Germans have a word Schaudenfreude, which means rejoicing in the misfortune of others. The Australians talk about Tall Poppy

Syndrome, the need to prove that someone who we put on a pedestal has feet of clay. The Irish use the word begrudgery to describe the need to bad-mouth anyone who achieves a certain level of success.

> *"Whenever a friend succeeds, a little something in me dies."*
> Gore Vidal

Bono (of U2 fame) illustrates the Irish attitude in story of his first visit to Beverly Hills. He was being shown around by his American host, who prized individualism and romanticised the maverick figure of the mythic entrepreneur. They looked at a beautiful new house up on a hill. There was a magnificent sports car outside, and by the side of a huge swimming pool stood the owner with a beautiful girl at his side. "See that guy," said the American friend. "He built himself up from nothing, and now look what he's achieved." But Bono remembers thinking to himself: "Why has that bastard got all this and I don't?"

BAD THING 2: NO REGULAR SALARY

When you worked in the ladder world, there were few surprises about money. You knew in advance what you earned, and you knew each month that your salary would appear in your bank account.

As an entrepreneur, especially in the early days, you don't know from day to day what your cash flow is going to be. Money that you are relying on ("I personally authorised payment last week") doesn't materialise. Sometimes, you will never see the money owed to you.

Clients can go bankrupt. They can disappear. Some simply refuse to pay. Recourse to the courts can prove to be more expensive than the sum owed. Some unscrupulous clients know this and exploit it. And in the meantime, you are being pressured by your suppliers and the bank to pay them what you are owed. Not to mention your employees waiting for their salaries.

My advice: Be careful. If you have even the slightest doubt about a client's ability to pay, demand a down payment. Don't let any client get too big - many small suppliers go under when a major client cancels orders.

BAD THING 3: COLLECTING DEBTS

In the ladder world, collecting money due was someone else's job. You did your work, someone else chased the client for payment. As an entrepreneur, collecting money owed is your lifeline. Suddenly, it's your responsibility to persuade clients to pay you for the work you did. And you will swiftly discover that not everyone shares your ideas of fairness.

You cannot afford not to give it high priority. If you think you'd be too embarrassed to chase up debts owed you, then adjust your backbone. Remember: This is business, not personal. They are sitting on your money. It is yours by right. It is illegal for them to deny you your money.

BAD THING 4: BEING SICK

When ladder people don't feel well, they stay at home. They get a doctor's note. They get sick leave – which is often paid for. The department and the company will survive when they are not there.

When you become an entrepreneur, you will learn to regard "not feeling well" as something to fear. You'll be torn between wanting to work and wanting to rest. You'll find yourself battling between the urge to sleep it off and the urge to get up and work.

Be careful. Ignoring health problems can boomerang on you. You may be better off absenting yourself for 3 days than to be at half-strength for 3 weeks.

BAD THING 5: VACATIONS

In the ladder world, you get paid vacations. As an entrepreneur, you get only what you give yourself. And that is often too little. You'll feel that there's something wrong about taking time off. You'll feel that taking a vacation from your own business is like stealing from the family piggy bank.

In the ladder world, except in exceptional circumstances, you can be sure that on national holidays you won't be working.

As an entrepreneur, you'll be happy when it's quiet and the phones aren't ringing. It's an opportunity to sort out all those things that have piled up. Your workload doesn't disappear on national holidays. It is very tempting to use the time to catch up.

BAD THING 6: SPENDING DECISIONS

In the ladder world, big questions about spending priorities were taken by someone else in the company. If your department needed a new software package costing a thousand dollars, you put in an application, it was approved, and you received it.

All of a sudden, these decisions are yours. You realise that there's never a good time to spend money. But some decisions can't be put off - and you'll have to take the plunge anyway.

BAD THING 7: LONELINESS

This is the biggie. This is numero uno. When you start your own business, you will suddenly feel very alone.

This sense of loneliness and isolation is common to just about everyone who makes the leap off the ladder to become their own boss. It is a theme that my seminar participants never fail to articulate, and it is a theme replicated in study after study across the world.

Whether we are talking about people who have just started out, or those who have been in business for years, the feedback is consistent. Loneliness can be the number one problem they encounter.

This loneliness is all the more problematic because it is so unexpected. The sense of isolation felt by people who run their own business often comes as a shock. No one warned them. They were not mentally prepared. However much we think we are ready to do everything on our own, however much we believe that we understand the meaning of "the buck stops here," the feeling of loneliness can catch us unawares.

Why is this?

The main reason is that in the ladder world, we are used to being part of a team. On a bad day, we have a colleague's shoulder to cry on. On a good day, there is always someone around to congratulate us. We have colleagues with whom to share things with. We are used to seeking - and receiving - validation from others. And when we get home, we can draw on further sympathy.

But this changes dramatically when you jump off the ladder.

Let's say you have a problem in your new business. Your automatic response might be to share this problem with former work colleagues. So you arrange to meet them after work. After exchanging pleasantries, you start explaining your problem.

Watch their eyes glaze over.

They won't want to know. They don't understand the world of self-employment, and they don't understand why you deserted them in the first place. You realise that you can no longer expect much understanding from that particular support system.

You won't fare much better at home. As we will see in a later chapter, your family is still trying to get their head around your decision to go it alone. It is not difficult to imagine the reception you are likely to receive from your loved one when you announce that the cheque you deposited yesterday - and that covers the mortgage payments and other standing orders - has bounced.

So what is the antidote to the loneliness of the long-distance entrepreneur?

For starters, stop blaming all those who cannot or do not support you. Seek out others who are guaranteed to speak your language. Seek out other entrepreneurs who have walked the entrepreneurial walk, who have survived the traumas of starting up on their own. If you want to counter the loneliness and sense of isolation that is the entrepreneur's lot, seek out others in the same boat.

When you want to moan, complain and bitch about clients, suppliers, the taxman and the bank, you can be sure that other entrepreneurs will understand. They will console you when business is bad, and they will affirm that it's normal to worry about your business.

"When I opened my business after being fired as the head of marketing, I was prepared for the fear of doing it on my own. But I wasn't prepared for the loneliness, especially in the first year. I hadn't realized how much support you get. When I warn people how lonely it is, they get this look of disbelief. 'Wait until that first time you find you've got no one to count on, and you'll see,' I tell them."
Timothy F. McCarthy, Sales Building Systems

Julia had been a self-employed ceramic artist for several years. Her business was thriving, and everything was fine - but she was having difficulty coping with the loneliness. Desperate for positive reinforcement, Julia had hit upon a solution. "Every couple of months, I phone a friend of mine in Paris who runs her own art gallery. All I need to hear are three magic words: 'Julia, you're wonderful.' It's my regular fix of emotional support. This feedback keeps me going for the next few weeks."

Sometimes, loneliness can tempt even long-term entrepreneurs back on to the ladder. Some years back, after 20 years as a freelance entrepreneur, I was asked to manage the PR department of a large company. The offer came during a period when the burdens of single-handedly carrying sole responsibility for my business weighed particularly heavily on me. For about a week, I was seriously tempted. Luckily, I resisted the temptation. I know for certain that it would have ended in tears.

Case Study

Jim ran his own office machines business. Over the years, he and a few other business owners in the town would meet up every Friday evening. They always went to the same pub and sat around the same table, chatting about their week. One Friday, as the group were swapping stories around the table, the local bank manager Philip happened to come into the same pub. Out of courtesy, and because most of the group knew him, Philip was invited to join the crowd around the table. Within minutes, the conversation dried up. The buzz that marked the weekly get-together fizzled out.

When Jim described this embarrassing incident to a networking group I was running, he interpreted what had happened. "We are a bunch of self-employed entrepreneurs who have naturally gravitated to one another. We all speak the same language. So when a ladder person joined the chat, we ran out of things to say. We were all too aware that Philip does not speak our language."

Here is some sound advice from idea2inception.com on how to battle loneliness: Don't be a businessman with everyone. For instance, wear the boyfriend (girlfriend) hat when you're with your girlfriend or wife (boyfriend or husband). With friends, be a friend first and then a businessman. Remember they befriended you and not what you do. Don't talk only about your business while on dinners, and parties. Talk about them too; ask them how have they been, or what's going on in their lives. Not to say that you shouldn't talk about your business or keep secrets but understand and respect the fact that not everyone is interested in your business, and may not be as excited as you.

I cannot offer you easy solutions to the bad things that can happen to entrepreneurs, and I certainly don't want to offer meaningless clichés. But you do need to look at these issues and ask yourself whether you have the mental, physical and financial resources to handle the problems of being your own boss.

CHAPTER 11
Hats off to entrepreneurs

"Running a start-up company is like being a juggler with a thousand different balls in the air. You can't let any of them drop."
Michael Stern, cofounder, Aquarium Ventures

One of the first things you learn when you start your own business is to become a juggler. You have to be prepared to wear any hat. If you work alone, you will have to juggle even more hats for even longer. Here are just some of the hats you will have to wear:

• CEO/Managing Director	• Payroll clerk	• Personnel manager
• PA to the CEO	• Company spokesman	• Customer support manager
• Telephonist	• Head of PR	• Recruitment officer
• Receptionist	• IT manager	• Business manager
• Sales manager	• Production manager	• New business manager
• Marketing director	• Warehouse manager	• Training manager
• Advertising manager	• Complaints manager	• Property manager
• Financial director	• Safety Manager	• Janitor
• Office manager	• R&D manager	• Canteen manager
• Strategist	• Handyman	• Maintenance manager
• Chief buyer		

The purpose of itemising these hats is not to frighten you off. But it's food for thought. At any given time, you will be wearing one or more hats. In the space of a few seconds, you will switch hats several times. Imagine the following scenario.

A prospective client comes to visit your one-person office. You welcome him, offer him coffee, and sit down to chat. He asks you questions about your service or product, prices, delivery times, and so on. While you are talking, you answer a call from someone enquiring about an ad you placed for a position in your new company. As you put the phone down, the room is plunged into darkness. While you're fixing the bulb, your new business cards are delivered.

In that sequence, how many hats did you wear? Let's re-run the scenario:

A prospective client comes to visit your one-man office. You welcome him (RECEPTIONIST), offer him coffee (CANTEEN MANAGER), and sit down to chat (CEO). You answer questions about your service or product (SALES PERSON, MARKETING MANAGER), prices (FINANCIAL DIRECTOR), delivery times (PRODUCTION MANAGER), and so on (CUSTOMER CARE MANAGER). While you are talking, you answer a call (PERSONAL ASSISTANT) from someone answering your ad (ADVERTISING MANAGER) for a position in your new company (HR MANAGER). As you put the phone down, the room is plunged into darkness, and you apologise to your guest (COMPANY SPOKESPERSON). While you're fixing the bulb (JANITOR), your new business cards (PR MANAGER) are delivered (GOODS IN).

15 hats - and all in just 5 minutes.

The good news is that you become adept at juggling the hats, and often feel a sense of pride in being able to master this particular skill.

CHAPTER 12
The myth of family support

In her book "Entrepreneurship for Dummies," Kathleen Allen states boldly: "You need the support of your family."

In his article "Are You Cut Out to Be an Entrepreneur?" in the Baltimore Business Journal, Harry Plack says: "Your family members and other individuals who depend on you must wholeheartedly support your endeavour."

In her article "The Delicate Balance of Work and Family" in Entrepreneur's Start-Up Magazine, Karen E. Spaeder says: "Don't go walking out onto that start-up tightrope without the support of loved ones to steer you in the right direction."

In her article "10 Tips to Help Conquer your Start-Up Fears - Making The Leap," in Business Start-Ups Magazine, Lynn H. Colwell says: "While family and friends may not be able to relate to your specific fears about starting a business, you should be able to count on them for emotional support."

In her Small Business Guide, Sara Williams tells us that our families: "... will have to understand that the home atmosphere should be very supportive. With a family, deciding to found an enterprise is likely to be more successful as a family decision."

In "Work for Yourself and Reap the Rewards," Brian Isaacs says: "The budding entrepreneur must have the full support of their family. Without their backing, you are not firing on all pistons."

I once attended a Personal Enterprise roadshow, which had dozens of huge panels containing stories and tips for the aspiring entrepreneur.

On one panel, I read:

"Indeed, we'd go so far as to say that you shouldn't even consider the possibility of starting a business unless your family wholeheartedly supports your decision to start a business."

There's only one problem with such platitudes.

They are wrong.

Dangerously wrong.

I believe that it is a myth that families can deliver the level of support that the wannabe entrepreneur craves. I believe that the broad coalition of opinion regarding support from family – a theme that is repeated in countless books, articles, websites and training courses – is based on wishful thinking, not on reality.

When the urge to start your own business first strikes you, it is human nature to want to share the good news with your nearest and dearest. As you rush home to tell them that you are giving up your salaried job to start your own business, you know what you want to hear from them:

- Great!
- You're my hero.
- I'm with you all the way.
- Fantastic.
- I knew you had it in you.
- How can I help?
- Your talents were wasted working for someone else.

Yes, there are a few – precious few - individuals who do indeed hear such responses. I have met some of them. Trust me when I say that these individuals are an endangered species. In reality, a very different response awaits most people in this situation. Instead of receiving congratulations and expressions of support, most people are subjected to downright hostility. Over the years, I have categorised these hostile reactions into 4 categories:

Category 1: QUESTIONING YOUR MENTAL HEALTH	Category 2: OUTRAGE
<ul><li>Are you nuts?</li><li>You're crazy.</li><li>You're out of your mind.</li><li>That's insane.</li><li>You need your head examined.</li><li>You need a psychiatrist.</li><li>You're emotionally unstable.</li><li>You're having a nervous breakdown.</li></ul>	<ul><li>How dare you!</li><li>You've got some nerve!</li><li>You arrogant bastard/bitch!</li><li>How could you be so irresponsible?</li><li>What about the mortgage?</li><li>What about the children's education?</li><li>What about our European vacation?</li></ul>
Category 3: PUT-DOWN	Category 4: THREAT/ULTIMATUM
<ul><li>Stop kidding yourself.</li><li>Get real.</li><li>You'll never make it.</li><li>Typical of you to think only of yourself.</li><li>Here you go again with another bee in your bonnet.</li><li>You don't have what it takes to be your own boss.</li></ul>	<ul><li>Over my dead body.</li><li>I don't want to hear another word of this nonsense.</li><li>No way.</li><li>Think again, buddy.</li><li>If you go ahead, I'm outta here.</li><li>Read my lips - no you're not.</li></ul>

This hostility is based on fear. It's not that your family doesn't **want** to support you. They are **incapable** of giving the emotional support that you want. Why? Because your family probably inhabits the ladder world. They have ladder values. They look at you through a fog of disbelief and incomprehension. They don't understand you. They feel threatened. They panic. And the more you are lulled into expecting support from people who cannot give it, the more disappointed you will be when this support is not forthcoming.

Case Study

In the early noughties, I was delivering an SYOB seminar in the San Diego Careers Center. As usual, I expounded my views on the myth of family buy-in. At the end of the seminar, Cindy, a 30-something web design student, came up and thanked me. I thanked her for the compliment, but she hadn't finished. "No, you don't understand. I'm thanking you because you've lifted a heavy weight from my shoulders. I first announced my intention of becoming a freelance web designer to my family two years ago. Their reaction was terrible. All my family and all my friends started treating me as if I'd lost it. Now know I'm normal. They're the ones who don't get it. This is the first time in 2 years that I don't feel like a freak. Thanks for liberating me."

Some spouses recognise that quashing a loved one's dream can lead to unhappiness and resentment. Meg Cadoux Hirshberg is the wife of Gary Hirshberg, president and CEO of Stonyfield Yogurt, the self-styled "pathological optimist" whose story appeared earlier as an example of resourcefulness.

In her regular column on the impact of entrepreneurial businesses on families, Meg asks rhetorically whether it's selfish to discourage a loved one from doing something they desperately want to do because it makes you uncomfortable. Or is it more selfish for them to persist in spite of your discomfort? She concludes that there is no easy answer.

Meg writes that she lives in terror of 4 little words: "I have an idea." Every time Gary utters these words, Meg says that the ground beneath her trembles. She quotes the wife of a repeat offender: "The personality of a serial entrepreneur is almost like a curse. They see opportunities every day."

Meg compares serial entrepreneurs to women who suppress the recollection of labour in order to marshal the stamina to give birth again.

I found this reader's letter in a business magazine I was leafing through in a dentist's office:

"Why does everyone praise the virtues of working 20 hours a day and getting no sleep? Why does no one write about the entrepreneur's spouse or partner going crazy (or worse - leaving the relationship) because the entrepreneur is never around? Why does no one write about the cost to the entrepreneur of not having a social life, not taking vacations, not engaging in any sort of physical exercise? I never read about an entrepreneur who sacrificed everything, including family, friends, and health, and was truly happy. I never read the story from the perspective of the spouse, partner, friend, or employee who bears the burden of dealing with irritable and cranky entrepreneurs. Entrepreneurs are in such a hurry to get to "someday" that they never stop to enjoy the moment. They go through years of pain and frustration before they realise that when someday arrives, it won't have been worth it."

There is some truth in these complaints. Entrepreneurs must somehow find a balance between their boundless enthusiasm and the need to look carefully at the other components of their life.

And in case anyone underestimates the seriousness of family hostility, the following case study will put you straight:

Case Study

After I delivered a Business Start-Up seminar in Dublin, I received the following email from Justin: Hello Yanky, I attended your seminar this evening. I have had a successful career in financial services. I'm 35, and I'm good at what I do. I have risen speedily up the corporate ladder, but now I have ants in my pants. I have a business idea that I know will succeed. However, my fiancée Eileen, with whom I live in the house we bought together, is adamantly opposed to my entrepreneurial plans. So it was a huge relief this evening to hear you say that hostility is a more common reaction than support. For the first time in two years, I heard words of encouragement. For the first time since I started telling those close to me about my plans, I felt that someone understands me. However, my elation was spectacularly short-lived. As I arrived home, it was as if Eileen had sat in at your seminar, and had learnt the script that you described. Literally at the doorway, she delivered the proverbial ultimatum. 'Either you give up this crazy idea of yours, or we're through.' Please can I meet you to discuss my predicament?

When we met for coffee, Justin told me that since his email to me, it occurred to him that he had probably not explained his idea in sufficient detail, so he had sat his fiancée and her parents down and patiently walked them through the details of his business plan. However, this had had the opposite effect. Instead of being mollified, Eileen had become even more stridently antagonistic to the idea. I had to gently explain to Justin that he had made things worse. The last thing that family wants to hear is that you have really thought this through are serious about going through with your plans.

Justin is not unique in believing that if only he had handled his "entrepreneurial announcement" a little better, he would have encountered less hostility.

But it doesn't work that way. The more the family hears of the hair-brained scheme, the more worried they get, not the other way round. There is no happy end to the story of Justin and Eileen. They split up, sold the house, and Justin moved to New Zealand to follow his entrepreneurial dream.

Obviously, not every situation ends up as dramatically as Justin's.

So what is to be done?

I got a clue from a comment made by Lisa at the end of a seminar she attended with her wannabe entrepreneurial husband. "You're being unfair to the spouses of would-be entrepreneurs."

"How come?" I replied.

"Because I learned more about what makes my husband tick from your seminar in one hour this evening, than I learned from him in the 2 years he's been going on about this. Why isn't it compulsory for all partners to attend your Business Start-Up session together with their entrepreneurial loved ones? That way, there will be a lot fewer unhappy families."

Well, there's a novel thought. Maybe it would be therapeutic if families discovered that the situation they find themselves in is not unique to them. It might also reduce the guilt that many spouses undoubtedly feel about their less-than-enthusiastic reaction.

People with an entrepreneurial bee in their bonnet could borrow some tips from the area of negotiation. Remember that your goal is accommodation, not victory. It does not help your cause when you make your announcement of impending changes like the proverbial bull in a china shop.

Give some thought to the physical space in which you make your announcement. Consider a neutral venue where both of you can talk without feeling intimidated.

You also have to choose the right timing. Choose a time of day when both of you are fit for a fruitful discussion. Avoid times when you are tired. Trying to squeeze your entrepreneurial announcement into a 1-minute window between the end of the meal and getting the kids off to bed is asking for trouble.

The conclusion of any successful negotiations is a trade-off. You know what your goal is: to start our own business. The question you need to ask is: Can I sweeten the blow? Don't expect miracles, but if you want to avoid confrontation and conflict, think through in advance what concessions you are prepared to make.

Ultimately, though, the issue is not what the family has to say about your plans. The issue is: How are you going to cope with the lack of family support? How will you navigate your way past their hostility? Are you emotionally able to proceed with your dreams and your plans, even if your family are not 100% - or even 1% - behind you?

I have met lots of people who carried on regardless.

And I have met several people who could not face the hostility – and shelved their entrepreneurial plans.

There is no right and wrong. Every individual has to work this out for themselves.

CHAPTER 13

Are you the right age to start your own business?

People often ask me: "Am I the right age to be my own boss?"

This question assumes the existence of a lower age limit (30? 25? 20?) and an upper age limit (50? 60? 70?)

I found a statistic that in knowledge intensive sectors, the average age of entrepreneurs is 37.6 years. So is someone aged 37.5 years too young, and someone aged 37.7 over the hill?

Of course not.

Allow me to state categorically: the whole notion of a best age to start a business is ludicrous.

The best predictor of entrepreneurship is neither age nor money. It is inclination. Don't worry about "when." Just make sure that you develop the right mindset – whatever your age.

If we look for inspiration to Silicon Valley, it would be easy to equate entrepreneurship with youth. Think of Jobs, Dell, Gates, Yang and others who founded industry-changing companies while still in their twenties.

There is a perception that people take fewer risks as they get older.

"Absolutely never say to yourself, I'm too old, if you can convey your passion for what you are doing."
Janet Hanson, founder, Milestone Capital Management

Well, you can throw that old chestnut out the window. In a 2009 report entitled "The Coming Entrepreneurship Boom," the Ewing Marion Kauffman Foundation shows that the average age of entrepreneurs is higher than many would expect. It turns out that over the past decade in the USA, the highest rate of entrepreneurial activity belongs to the 55-64 age group. The 20-34 age bracket, usually identified with swashbuckling and risk-taking Google-style entrepreneurs, actually has the lowest rate.

Case Studies

- *Ben Casnocha started his first company when he was 12, was named entrepreneur of the year by* Inc *magazine at 17, and published a guide to running start-ups at 19.*

- *Harland Sanders started franchising Kentucky Fried Chicken when he was 65.*

- *Gary Burrell was 52 when he left Allied Signal to help start GPS giant Garmin.*

- *Harold S. Blue, chairman of Proxymed Inc., a health-care information services company in Ft. Lauderdale, Florida, was 10 years old when he started his first business, a neighbourhood snow removal service. At 16, he set up a drugstore in the lobby of a new, unrented doctors building, which soon brought in renters for the owner and led to a booming business for himself.*

- *School dropout Chester Greenwood was trying out his new ice skates when his ears got very cold from the icy wind. He fashioned two ear-shaped loops, and asked his grandmother to sew fur on them. The United States Patent Office awarded him patent #188,292 for the world's first ear-muffs. Greenwood went on to make a fortune supplying ear protectors to US soldiers during WW1.*

- When Mike Lloyd lost his job in his 60s, he saw an ad in a garden centre. A new florist wanted a driver. He got the job, and his first delivery was to a local undertaker. When he arrived, 3 separate florists' vans were also delivering flowers. He set up Flying Flowers Network, and was soon working with a dozen florists in the area.

- Doris Drucker, the wife of management guru Peter Drucker, was in her 80s when she got it into her head to start her first ever business. Together with friends, she developed the VISIVOX visual feedback monitor, which went on to sell in the hundreds. Today, the VISIVOX is even being used by speech pathologists who use the device to help people modulate their voice.

- By age 12, Michael Dell had established his own postage stamp mail order business with a turnover of thousands of dollars. In high school, he made $18,000 selling newspaper subscriptions. He turned his room in university into a PC upgrading workshop, which was soon pulling in $50,000 a month. He quit college, moved to an off-campus condo, and founded Dell Computer.

- 13-year-old schoolboy Dominic McVey was surfing the web when he came across Viza, the collapsible silver scooter manufacturer. He persuaded the manufacturer to appoint him as UK distributor, and by the age of 15, he was running a business with a turnover of several million pounds.

- When Ely Callaway reached his sixties, everyone expected him to play endless rounds of golf. But he didn't want to buy golf clubs. He wanted to make them. He founded Callaway Golf with just three employees, and over the next two decades, until he was well into his eighties, he turned his passion into a $6 billion business operation.

If there is one theme that emerges from all these case studies, it is that you can never be too old or too young to start your own business.

There is no "perfect" age to start on the road to business ownership. There are successful entrepreneurs aged 10 and successful entrepreneurs aged 90.

Age is no obstacle when someone is determined to succeed and has faith in their abilities.

Are you the right age to start your own business?

You bet!

CHAPTER 14

Is a recession a good time to start a business?

Yes. No. Maybe. *

* (For readers who want a slightly longer answer to this question, see over the page.)

I think that the pros and cons of starting your own business in a recession cancel each other out.

Just as age does not affect the timing of the entrepreneurial urge, the recession likewise has no direct influence. Naturally, job losses during a recession can force more people to consider the entrepreneurial option. But ultimately, you must want to be your own boss.

The downturn of the first decade of the noughties has posed another awkward question: Why did so many once-celebrated entrepreneurs turn out to be crooks? Newt Gingrich, former speaker of the US House of Representatives, has expressed his concern that entrepreneurs may now be asking themselves: "Why not get a nice, safe government job instead?"

In other words, has the recession put people off starting a new business?

Again, I think that this is the wrong question.

If you are determined to jump off the ladder, you will do so whatever the circumstances.

If you're too scared to jump off the ladder, the recession won't change your feelings.

CHAPTER 15
Don't Accept The Failure Label

"The most essential factor is the determination never to allow your energy or enthusiasm to be dampened by the discouragement that must inevitably come."
James Whitcomb Riley

When you start your own business, everyone suddenly has an opinion. People who themselves have failed in business are reborn as business experts. People who have never ever wanted to work on their own suddenly know all the perils of entrepreneurship.

Always remember that most of these people are ladder-centric. Their advice will come from their ladder experience.

Negativity is often just a projection of other people's agendas. There is no point trying to please everyone, even those close to you. Don't let anyone create doubt in your mind.

If the Wright Brothers had listened to the words of celebrated inventor Lord Kelvin: "I have not the smallest molecule of faith in aerial navigation" – they might never have gone on to perform the first-ever powered air flight.

George Orwell's *Animal Farm* was rejected by 23 publishers, including Faber and Faber. The rejection letter was signed by TS Eliot.

A former BBC news department journalist had his thriller manuscript rejected by a string of major publishers. WH Allen turned it down on the grounds of "No reader interest." Finally, Hutchinson agreed to take a chance on Frederick Forsyth's *The Day of the Jackal.*

*"When I was a young man, I observed that 9 out of 10
things I did were failures. I didn't want to be a failure,
so I did 10 times more work."*
George Bernard Shaw

Case Study

A year before I moved to Ireland, I had dinner with a top Dublin banker whom I'd been introduced to. I was not asking him for a loan, and in any case he was not in commercial banking. All I wanted was some advice about the business scene. I was also interested in his contacts. I explained the areas I planned to get into when I moved to Ireland. His response: "We have already invented the wheel in Ireland." The sub-text was clear. "You've nothing new to offer. You'll never get your business off the ground." Luckily, I also met with professionals in my field who encouraged me. I didn't let the banker's negativity discourage me.

If Norma Jean Baker had followed the advice of the Blue Book modelling agency, she would have become a secretary instead of becoming Marilyn Monroe.

"Cat in the Hat" author Theodor Geiselk, also known as Dr Seuss, who became one of the most prolific and famous children's authors of all time, had his first book rejected by 23 publishers.

While at Yale, FedEx founder Frederick W. Smith wrote a paper about a speedy and reliable national and international overnight passenger-less courier service based on air cargo. His economics professor was singularly unimpressed: "The concept is interesting and well-formed, but in order to earn better than a C, the idea must be feasible." Smith went on to create the world's first air courier company.

*"Keep away from people who try to belittle your ambitions.
Small people always do that."*
Mark Twain

Remember, failure is not an objective yardstick. Do not accept anyone else's definition. We only fail when we give up trying. The real test is how we handle failure and what we can learn from it.

Case Study

He drifted from job to job, and eventually opened a dry goods shop in Boston. When this failed, he joined the California Gold Rush, and opened another dry goods store. It folded. He returned to Massachusetts and opened another dry goods store. When this failed, he tried his luck in Superior City. This venture also failed, so he moved into real estate, and again he lost money. He moved to New York City, where he opened a small fancy goods store in a location where several other businesses had failed. Within two months, the store was robbed and there was a fire. But he never gave up. He gradually added new lines of merchandise, and eventually bought the surrounding stores. Despite all his business failures, Rowland Hussey Macy refused to accept the failure label.

"There are always people who haven't done anything who spend their lives warning others not to do anything."
Bernie Ecclestone

Just because you close your business does not mean that it has failed. Wrigley's began life as a soap manufacturer. When they used chewing gum as a promotion for their soap powder, they realised that they could make much more money selling chewing gum, so they eventually closed down their soap business. Was Wrigley's a failure?

Not being devastated by failure also means not beating yourself up for absolutely everything that happens. Some things really are out of your control. If you take the blame for everything, you'll be carrying the weight of the world on your shoulders.

Instead of forever saying to yourself: "Why did I do that?" "Why am I such an idiot?" – decide to learn a valuable lesson. There's no more powerful learning than the learning that comes from your own mistakes.

Case Study

He tried his hand at business but failed. He ran for the political office of State Legislature, and lost. He tried another business venture. Again he failed. He ran for political office once again, and was elected to the State Legislature. But when he ran for Speaker of the House, he lost. He was elected to Congress, but lost when he ran for a second term. A few years later, he ran for the US Senate. He failed to get elected. He ran for Vice President, and lost again. Two years later he tried again for US Senate, and failed once more. Two years later, he ran for the Presidency. The man who refused to accept the label "loser," who ignored failure, and who hung on to his dream, became the sixteenth President of the United States. The name of one of the most famous and influential people in world history? Abraham Lincoln.

Failure can be an important catalyst of change. In fact, many entrepreneurs feel sorry for people who have only experienced success, because they don't know the rewards of failure.

In the face of negative thinking, keep telling yourself that your instincts are healthy, that whatever you based your decision on is sound, no matter what Tom, Dick or Harriet has to say.

Protect your creative thoughts from people who tell you it won't work.

CHAPTER 16

Don't slam the door on the ladder world

There is a memorable scene in the movie *Jerry Maguire*. After Tom Cruise has been unceremoniously fired, he delivers a profanity-laden tirade against his boss and his co-workers.

Do not be tempted to emulate this behaviour – even if it did inspire Bridget Jones – sorry, Renee Zellweger – to follow him out of the building!

If you decide that you definitely want to leave your ladder job and start your own business, be smart.

Don't burn your bridges.

Don't slam the door.

Leave with dignity.

Exercise strategic and tactical thinking, and leave the door open for longer-term dialogue.

Just because you're leaving does not mean the relationship has to end. You never know when your paths might cross again. You might need the ladder and the ladder might need you. You could be called in as a consultant. You might be able to use their contacts.

So resist the temptation to make phone calls on company time – unless you square this first with your boss. Consider your re-entry strategy. You have nothing to lose by discussing a "What if....?" scenario with your employer.

However strong your gut feeling that you want to get off the ladder and start your own business, the reality of entrepreneurship can sometimes be very cruel. You may hit a run of bad luck. Things can go wrong. Cheques will bounce. You lose orders. You have a cash flow crisis that forces you to close the business.

You may have chosen the worst possible time to get off the ladder.

Seamus left his job as a driver for a large freight company to buy his own taxi. He paid €100,000 for the hard-to-come-by plates - just 2 months before government deregulation reduced their value to a few hundred euro. He was left with huge debts.

You may have chosen to go into a business that was undergoing rapid change.

Lisa left her ladder job to buy a stationery supply shop. She took out loans, she brought in members of the family, and she bought lots of stock. Two months later, a nationwide chain opened a new stationery superstore 50 yards down the road. Her turnover was decimated, and she had to close the business with heavy losses.

You may have liked the idea of owning a business more than the reality.

Geraldine bought the mini-market that she had previously managed. Soon after taking over the business, there was large scale theft by staff. She discovered that she had been more comfortable running the store on behalf of the owner, than owning the store herself. She sold the business at a loss, and found a job as spokesperson and fundraiser for an educational organisation. Geraldine has almost total autonomy in her new job, and she's happy she went back to the ladder world.

You may have become too reliant on a single client.

Eleanor left the large graphic design studio where she was employed in order to start her own design business. She moved off the ladder because she found a really big client. The workload was huge, and she took on a team of designers. Less than a year after opening her studio, her big client went into liquidation - and Eleanor was left with debts that forced her own business to fold.

Even if you have entrepreneurial blood streaming through your veins, you may not have a head for business.

Dave was a gifted chef. Encouraged by his success in supplying catered meals to friends, he decided to leave his newspaper job to start his own catering business. But he had no idea about pricing, and was charging less for his meals than they cost him to make. Within a short time, Dave had lost thousands, and the business folded.

You may discover that being your own boss does not automatically prepare you to be someone else's boss. Many entrepreneurs never had a "good boss" as a role model. On the contrary, their decision to jump off the ladder is often motivated by problems with managers and bosses. So how are you meant to know how a good boss behaves?

Jeremy had fantasies of running an international management consultancy, with offices worldwide. But he soon realised that he would have to trim his dreams – because he discovered that he was not very good at dealing with staff. He would get impatient. He would get frustrated. He was not comfortable in the role of boss. So he shelved his dreams of employing a cast of thousands. He now runs his international management consultancy alone.

You may conclude that however keen you are to run your own show, you don't want to be anyone else's boss – nor do you want to work alone. Whatever the reason, it's OK to cut your losses and hop back on the ladder.

Don't be too proud to take refuge in the ladder world while you lick your wounds.

Some of you will be scared off the entrepreneurial experience forever, and will vow never to try such foolishness again.

More of you are likely to keep an eye out for the next opportunity to jump off the ladder and once again try to be your own boss.

And some of you might end up jumping off and jumping back on the ladder world quite a few times in your life.

And that's OK too.

Remember, it's your decision. It's your life.

You can alternate between the ladder and non-ladder worlds as often as you want - until you find what you want.

Don't let anyone usurp your role in deciding what you should do.

INTRAPRANEURS:
A BIT ON THE LADDER, A BIT OFF THE LADDER

There is a perpetual fear in the ladder world that if ambitious employees aren't given more autonomy, they will leave and go into business on their own. One solution is to encourage the emergence of intrapreneurs.

An intrapreneur is someone within a large corporation who takes direct responsibility for turning an idea into a profitable finished product through assertive risk-taking and innovation. What usually happens is that a senior executive in a company champions a team of employees who want to push a particular idea.

Intrapreneurism can solve the dilemma for people with an independent streak who cannot bring themselves to take the plunge and start their own business. Being an intrapraneur can give you the confidence to take the leap and make a go of it on your own. Entrepreneurs are being enticed to rejoin the ladder to become intrapreneurs.

Several leading companies use intrapreneurship to promote innovation within their ranks. One of the most famous examples is 3M. Spencer Silver was working in the 3M research laboratories in 1970 trying to find a strong adhesive. He developed a new adhesive, but it was even weaker than what 3M already manufactured. It stuck to objects, but could easily be lifted off. It did not seem to have any practical use, but Silver didn't discard it. One Sunday, four years later, another 3M scientist named Arthur Fry was singing in his church choir. He used markers to keep his place in the hymnal, but they kept falling out of the book. He remembered Silver's discarded adhesive, and the weak adhesive was exactly what was needed. Fry became a champion of the adhesive, and he pushed and cajoled 3M to develop the Post-it Notes. The success of Fry's initiative encouraged 3M to initiate a policy of intrapreneurship that is now 3M's hallmark.

CHAPTER 17
Sprinkle Chutzpah On Your Endeavours

"Chutzpah builds the muscles of enterprise."
Allison Kalloo

You need a lot of nerve to want to start your own business. You need courage. You need balls. You need chutzpah - an evocative term which originates in ancient Aramaic but is now common currency in the USA and increasingly in English-speaking Europe. Chutzpah is a combination of verve, cheek, daring and audacity.

The Economist defines chutzpah as "that upbeat sense of self-confidence that says anything is possible, go for it, and never be too shy to ask for help."

Entrepreneur Magazine defines chutzpah as "daring to dream, facing fears, taking risks, finding balance, giving back, growing new eyes and laughing at life."

Inc.com claims that it is possible to bootstrap a company – and thrive – by using "ingenuity, doggedness and chutzpah."

On her website, Oprah she describes the attributes of the women who have been chosen to receive the Oprah Chutzpah Awards: "Meet nine women whose chutzpah - audacity, nerve, boldness, conviction - has taken them to the most amazing places."

"The really successful people I know all have chutzpah and are proud of it. I believe my personal success comes from having the guts, the nerve, and the no fear attitude which allows me to live fully, freely and without fear."
Terri Levine, Comprehensive Coaching U

You need chutzpah to believe you can make it on your own.

You need chutzpah - and guts - to get off the ladder.

You need chutzpah - and courage - to embark on a new venture with no guarantee that it will succeed.

You need chutzpah to try and compete with established companies in your field.

You need chutzpah to approach your potential customers with no record or background, and to convince them that they should buy whatever goods or services you are selling.

> *"I firmly believe in chutzpah - that terrific Yiddish word for gall, guts, the drive to put yourself ahead."*
> Helen Gurley Brown

I've been told that it takes chutzpah to walk around with a name like Yanky Fachler. My wife Mona's first words to me when she spotted the name Yanky on my name tag were: "Your mother has a lot to answer for!" Like Ben Stiller's Fokker character in *Meet the Parents*, my surname has always been the source of much merriment. Once, in West Cork, I was introduced to an audience as Yanky Faulkner.

On my first day in boarding school, someone said: "Hey, new boy, what's your name?" In my innocence, I proudly informed him that it was Yanky Fachler. He hastened to inform all his companions that Wanky Fuckler had arrived at the school. I understood neither word, but I quickly decided that for the duration of my boarding school career, I would be Jack. And Jack I was for the next 7 years.

I have been told that if I'd have paid a fortune to a branding company to come up with a brand name for myself, they could never have produced anything as distinctive as my own name!

Case Study

Soon after Cliff Hardcastle opened an import-export operation, he was asked by Thorn EMI Defence Division to supply digital displays. The buyer urgently needed an outside source, mistakenly believing that the Thorn division which made the displays had ceased production. Cliff discovered that the Thorn display plant had not ceased production, but it had relocated to a new site 200 miles away. So Cliff went to the plant, obtained a quote for the displays, added 30% to the price, and went back to the buyer who promptly placed a big order.

Cliff sold Thorn products to Thorn.

"The single biggest reason most businesses fail is the lack of chutzpah when needed. Successful business owners all share a healthy cynicism, insecurity and chutzpah."
Cliff Ennico

Case Study

Alex Trew enrolled as a mature student to study business management in Nottingham University. He was broke, and was about to take on over £20,000 debt to cover his fees. He asked himself: 'How can I come up with an idea that was simple to understand and to set up; that would attract media interest;and has a good name?"

He created a website called the Million Dollar Homepage on which he sold one million pixels (the tiny dots that make up an image on a screen) at $1 per pixel. Each of the 10,000 boxes of pixels contained the advertiser's logo, which, when clicked on, transported web users to the customers' own site. Alex sold the first 10 boxes, and used the $1,000 on a press release that was picked up by the BBC. News of his exploits spread virally. Instead of £20,000, he raised over £500,000.

Use your chutzpah to defy conventional wisdom, to zigzag around the doors that won't open, and to bend and change the rules.

Use your chutzpah to shamelessly seek out anyone who can help you achieve your goals, and to stretch the boundaries of your creative imagination.

Case Study

Dublin's roads are notorious for being almost permanently choked with traffic. The only vehicles that can move relatively freely and avoid the gridlock are the buses and taxis that travel in the dedicated bus lanes. As he made the daily commute from his native Mullingar, a provincial town, to his office in Dublin Airport, Ryanair's flamboyant CEO Michael O'Leary used to look enviously at the taxis overtaking him on the inside lane. So he bought a taxi plate (license), hired a cab driver, and became the taxi company's main (and only) passenger. This exploitation of a legal loophole left the National Taxi Drivers Federation and business executive rivals screaming about unfair tactics. O'Leary laughed it all off as sour grapes. Insisting that he was complying fully with the law, he managed to keep a straight face while claiming that he had simply bought the taxi as a good investment. The story dominated the Irish airwaves and print media for weeks, and it took a full two years before the loophole was plugged.

When Oak Tree Press first published *Fire in the Belly*, I decided to launch the book locally. I had never actually been to a book launch, but it didn't seem like rocket science. Since I didn't have any spare funds to finance the launch, I resorted to chutzpah.

I used chutzpah to persuade the County Museum that the launch of a book by a local author was an event of public importance, and that they should therefore waive their fee. I used chutzpah to persuade a client who produced smoked salmon to provide the eats for the event.

I used chutzpah to persuade another client to donate the wine. I used chutzpah to persuade the Chamber of Commerce to make this an official chamber event and to circulate an invitation to all members. I used chutzpah to persuade the organisers of the local drama festival to feature the launch in their official list of events.

I used chutzpah to persuade the drama festival MC (later my wife!) to announce the launch from the stage. I used chutzpah to persuade my bank manager that the bank should also contribute to the cost of the launch.

I used chutzpah to persuade an event management client to provide huge clowns to greet the guests. I used chutzpah to persuade the local media to feature the launch.

The upshot of this multiple chutzpah, as reported in the local press, was that well before the advertised time of the launch, a record crowd of about 200 squeezed into the museum. Alan Clark, who had first pushed me in the direction of Business Start-Up, came over from Scotland in his kilt to be the MC. I sold over 100 books, and my publishing career was well and truly launched.

"A little chutzpah is a vital element in every entrepreneur's toolkit."
Ed Zimmer

Shortly after starting her business, 27-year-old Maria Carilao, founder of Yo-Bonic Yo-Yos in Seattle, gained the attention of premier specialty toy retailer FAO Schwarz by tying her "yo-yos with an attitude" to the doors of its New York City store along with dozens of her business cards. "I wanted the top-notch stores to sell my product, so I did whatever it took to get their attention," explained Carilao, the world's first CEyO.

Encourage your chutzpah genie to escape. Nurture your chutzpah spark. Believe in your own chutzpah. Own it.

Every entrepreneur has chutzpah - it's in our DNA. You need to reclaim your chutzpah.

Case study

After completing his professional training as a chef, Russell Morgan spent several years working in Hilton Hotels around the world before establishing his own full service catering company. Hungry to expand his fledgling business, he was constantly on the lookout for an opportunity to break into the big time.

One day, he read an article in the Catering Times about Brigadier Kit Barclay, the man responsible for commissioning catering companies for government functions. Barclay was quoted as saying that government hospitality enjoyed the services of the three finest providers of food in London. Russell wrote to the brigadier. "There has to be some mistake. You cannot be using the top three food companies, otherwise you would be employing my company."

The brigadier invited Russell to meet him in his plush Central London offices, gave him a commission to cater for an event in Lancaster House, and Russell ended up with a 10-year contract to provide the catering for No. 10 Downing Street.

Is chutzpah any guarantee of success? No.

Earlier, we described how Barney the dinosaur had managed to deliver Yossi Abramowitz's business plan to the desk of the business angel from whom he was requesting funding. But when the CEO read the business plan, he rejected it as completely non-feasible. So Yossi used more chutzpah to access another angel – and this time he got the funding he wanted.

Chutzpah is a permanent state of mind. Sprinkle it liberally on all your business endeavours.

CHAPTER 18
Fire In The Belly

Get excited and enthusiastic about your own dream.
This excitement is like a forest fire –
you can smell it, taste it, and see it from a mile away.
Denis Waitley

Whether you're a born entrepreneur or a late entry into the entrepreneurial world, once you get the idea into your head that you are going to start your own business, the main thing you will need is fire in the belly.

Fire in the belly is the fuel that drives your enterprise.

Fire in the belly launches you into a whole new stratosphere.

With fire in your belly, you are invincible.

With fire in your belly, you can turn the zaniest idea into a workable business proposition.

With fire in the belly, you have the right tools to embark on your entrepreneurial odyssey.

You will need loads and loads of passion and fire in the belly to help you nurture your new business.

"I can instinctively tell the difference between people who have
fire in their belly and those who see their ideas primarily
as a way to get rich."
Venture capitalist Arthur Rock

There can be no half measures when you start a new business. If you can't give it total commitment, don't start. If you don't have fire in your belly, your business will not succeed.

Ever since the publication of the first edition of *Fire in the Belly*, I have been asked, why fire in the **belly**? Why not fire in the **brain**, or fire in the **heart**?

The answer of course is that the decision to start your own business is not merely a rational or intellectual decision fuelled by logic, strategy or money. The decision is an emotional one.

The belly is the seat of our emotions. That's where our guts are. That's where we feel the butterflies in our stomach.

> *"Motivation is a fire from within. If someone else tries to light that fire under you, chances are it will burn very briefly."*
> Stephen R. Covey

In this book, we defined an entrepreneur as anyone who feels the urge to be their own boss and who starts their own business.

We defined the Ladder World as the world of employment where a regular salary defines the workplace relationship.

We looked at why some employees come to regard the ladder world as a health hazard, and are no longer prepared to hop from one ladder to another.

We examined the triggers that can push you and pull you off the ladder, and we discussed the process of choosing in which business field to make your mark.

We itemised the prerequisites for starting your own business, and we drew comparisons between the ladder and the non-ladder worlds.

We looked at some of the fun things associated with going it alone, and we looked at the sense of loneliness and other problems that can cast a shadow on the entrepreneurial life.

We congratulated the entrepreneur's ability to wear so many hats, and we challenged the myth of universal family buy-in.

We dismissed the notion that you need to be a particular age to start your own business, and we engaged in a lengthy debate over whether a recession is a good time to become an entrepreneur.

We cautioned against accepting other people's definitions of failure, we looked at why you should make an elegant exit from the ladder world. We urged you to use chutzpah wherever you can.

"I never could stand losing. Second place didn't interest me.
I had a fire in my belly."
Ty Cobb

If you follow the advice I have so freely dished out in this book, you will have effectively conducted a sort of **Fire in the Belly Emotional Fitness Audit** on yourself.

You will have a better appreciation of what being your own boss is about. You'll know more about the pain and more about the gain.

And if you believe that you can successfully navigate the mental transition from ladder think to entrepreneur think, the hard part is already behind you.

Now comes the easier part. Bridge your skills deficit. Read inspiring business books. Attend Business Start-Up training courses. Visit entrepreneurship websites. Seek professional advice. Hire people with the skills you lack. Immerse yourself in entrepreneurial pursuits. Be inspired by the stories of other entrepreneurs. Join networks of other entrepreneurs.

In your dealings with banks and other ladder people, never forget that you embrace a different belief system from them. Calm them down a little by learning their vocabulary.

And throughout your entrepreneurial pursuits, don't forget that a little chutzpah goes a long way.

Whatever you do, don't be discouraged by others who lack your vision, lack your drive, lack your passion.

Remember, the best thing about fire in the belly is that all the fire trucks in the world cannot extinguish it.

Stick to your guns, and go for it.

Good luck!

"Fire in the belly comes from pride and passion."
Soccer manager Bill Shankly

About the author

Broadcaster, corporate trainer, motivational speaker and author Yanky Fachler is an internationally acclaimed expert in the Business Start-Up field. His innovative use of his trademark step-ladder in his "Do I have what it takes?" seminars has earned him a legion of fans.

Yanky leverages his stage background to bring energy, enthusiasm and humour to his keynotes, workshops, seminars and talks. His corporate training expertise has been influenced by his long record of involvement in marketing communication campaigns worldwide. He has written literally thousands of ads, websites, commercials, speeches, brochures, slogans, reports, press releases, packaging texts, narration scripts and PPT presentations.

Yanky is also a conference facilitator, speaking coach, and a much-in-demand motivational speaker who has addressed audiences in Ireland, the USA, the UK, Poland and the Czech Republic. He makes frequent TV and radio appearances, he has a monthly column in *BusinessPlus Magazine,* and writes Yanky's Biz Book Blog on www.bookbuzz.biz. Hundreds of his articles have appeared in newspapers, magazines and journals including *Business & Finance* and *The Irish Independent.*

Yanky is CEO of High Octane Communications, and co-founder and Chief Learning Officer of Bookbuzz Executive Development. He lives in Ireland with his wife Mona, and he is the proud father of sons Ashi and Amiti, and grandfather to Uri, Nissan and Gilli.

yanky@eircom.net   353-86-8575162

PS from the cover designer

Hi, I'm Yanky's son, Ashi, a photographer/graphic designer living in San Diego, California. While my dad was visiting me in Southern California, we were talking about the photo we wanted on the back cover of the book. I organized a photoshoot (see www.flickr.com/ashi for more of my photos,) and while moving from location to location, I spotted a yellow Ferrari near Dana Point Harbor. I knew this was the shot I wanted. I asked my dad to lean on the car with a "Hey Yes! As a matter of fact I DO own it!" look on his face. (Which is very amusing, since he has never really been into cars.)

"Yellow Ferrari?" I hear you ask. "But the Ferrari on the cover is red." Well, thank you Photoshop! (Please don't tell my dad that the Ferrari is red. He's color blind, and probably thinks that the Ferrari on the cover is yellow.) "But," I hear you persist, "the license plate reads YANKY." OK, so I took poetic license. As a designer, it's my job to deliver a visual that will make people pick up the book and say "I want to be like that!" And if I have to change a colour here, personalize something there, nip and tuck a little (sorry dad) - so be it!

Incidentally, the original license plate read "VIDGAMES" and it is truly my hope that the owner bought his Ferrari from the proceeds of a spectacularly successful video-games-development startup.

Enjoy the book. Let the fire in your belly guide you through the entrepreneurial labyrinth, and remember that the right time to start your own business is when you're ready.

You may have noticed that at my insistence, the font for this page is not Comic Sans. Ban Comic Sans, I say. Visit http://bancomicsans.com/main/

Yanky's Corporate Training Courses

- Do I have what it takes to start my own business?
- The emotional transition from employee to self-employed
- Idea generation – coming up with innovative ideas
- Marketing on a shoestring
- Pigeons and statues – the entrepreneur's roller-coaster ride
- Chutzpah in business
- Networking skills
- Customer service
- Personal impact
- Personal effectiveness
- Communications skills
- Presentation skills
- Public speaking skills
- PowerPoint skills
- Business writing skills
- Press release writing skills
- Minute taking skills

yanky@eircom.net 353-86-8575162